POPULAR CULTURE AND POLITICAL IDENTITY

IN THE ARAB GULF STATES

Other Titles in the Series

SOAS MIDDLE EAST ISSUES

Popular Culture and Political Identity
in the Arab Gulf States

Edited by
Alanoud Alsharekh & Robert Springborg

SAQI

in association with

**LONDON
MIDDLE EAST
INSTITUTE
SOAS**

ISBN: 978-0-86356-692-9

© London Middle East Institute at SOAS, 2008

The publication of this book was generously supported by Air Products Plc.

A full CIP record for this book is available from the British Library.

A full CIP record for this book is available from the Library of Congress.

Manufactured in Lebanon

SAQI

26 Westbourne Grove, London W2 5RH
825 Page Street, Suite 203, Berkeley, California 94710
Tabet Building, Mneimneh Street, Hamra, Beirut
www.saqibooks.com

in association with

The London Middle East Institute

School of Oriental and African Studies, Russell Square, London WC1H 0XG
www.lmei.soas.ac.uk

Contents

Acknowledgments

This book and the conference upon which it is based would not have been possible without the assistance and generous support of various individuals and institutions. Her Royal Highness Princess Fadwa Bint Khaled of the Royal Embassy of the Kingdom of Saudi Arabia in London not only participated in the planning of the event, but provided to it the generous assistance of the Women's Section of that embassy and its capable head, Dr Elham Danish, and her staff. The director of the Kuwait Information Agency in London, Khaled al Tarrah, provided valuable advice and assistance and contributed substantial material support from the centre. Richard Muir, former UK Ambassador to Kuwait and Oman, served as a key member of the organising committee, offering valuable advice throughout the long planning process. Sir Harold Walker, former UK Ambassador to Iraq, spoke eloquently on the subject of culture and identity at the conference dinner.

The publication of this book was made possible through the financial support of Air Products plc, whose Vice President for the Middle East, Richard Boocock, was enthusiastically engaged in both the planning of the conference and the book from the outset.

Louise Hosking, Executive Officer of the London Middle East Institute, copyedited the entire manuscript, greatly improving it in the process. The staff at Saqi Books and especially its commissioning editor, Lara Frankena, went above and beyond the call of duty in helping to produce the book.

The editors would like to thank all of these individuals and organisations for having made this volume possible.

Introduction

Robert Springborg

This book is the product of two conferences on the Gulf organised by the London Middle East Institute. The first, held in February 2005, was devoted to the changing nature of family and kinship in the countries of the Gulf Cooperation Council and gave rise to an earlier publication in the SOAS Middle East Issues series, *The Gulf Family*. Discussion in the final session of that conference about what topic would be most compelling for a follow-on event revealed that the GCC citizens present favoured a conference that would highlight Gulf culture. They expressed a desire that the world be made aware of the fact that the Gulf did indeed have its own distinctive culture which was founded in traditional practices and social organisation, but which was evolving rapidly in tune with the rapid modernisation of the region. They emphasised that Gulf culture is distinguishable from other Middle Eastern cultures, hence needs to be appreciated and analysed in its own right and not as some derivative form.

It was clear that the sentiments expressed were heartfelt, reflecting a certain disappointment and possibly even resentment that the rest of the world, including other parts of the Middle East, has tended to be dismissive of indigenous Gulf culture. Indeed, this seems well founded, as suggested by the coexistence of mutually exclusive stereotypes of Gulf culture. One view is that the Gulf is a backward region in which inadequate education, easy wealth, male dominance and persistence of tribalism have militated against cultural dynamism, so traditional cultural norms and practices persist. A contrasting view is that the region is super modern, with the rapid pace of globalisation having thoroughly undermined traditional culture, replacing it with a cosmopolitan, international one in which women are leading the way. A negative view that combines these two opposites suggests that traditional culture has essentially been destroyed while a modern one has yet to take root, so the Gulf is essentially without culture. Small surprise, then, that citizens of the Gulf feel misunderstood and misrepresented, even in the Middle East, to say nothing of the world beyond.

A decision was thus reached at that conference to organise a follow-on event, which was duly held in February 2007 under the title *Popular Culture and Political Identity in the Arab Gulf States*. The central aim was to reflect the diversity of Gulf culture while investigating its sources, pressures for change and its articulation with authority structures, most importantly that of states. Topics were chosen that would address several key points. First, it was deemed important to convey the sense of how close the Gulf is to its pre-modern past and what efforts are being made to connect citizens to that past. The volume commences with an overview by Fred Lawson and Hasan al-Naboodah of steps taken by the government in the UAE to preserve and project that country's cultural heritage, which the authors see as exemplifying an initial stage in the development and articulation of nationalism. In the living memory of many of its citizens, Gulf economies were based on pearling, trade, fishing and agriculture, with social units organised around those functions. Reflections by UAE elders contained in the chapter by Nadia Rahman and based on an extensive oral-history project in the UAE described also by Lawson and Naboodah, as well as reflections on pearl diving in Kuwait found in Sulayman Khalaf's contribution, provide ample evidence of both the nearness of those pasts as well as their almost complete submersion by rapid socioeconomic change.

A closely related topic was that of how states seek to foster collective memories of common origins and general appreciation of shared pasts so as to reinforce and anchor sovereignty in 'imagined communities'. Cultural-heritage preservation programmes for material culture are examples of such state-led efforts, as Mohammed Alkhozai's chapter indicates in the case of Bahrain. Sulayman Khalaf's just-mentioned chapter is based on an endeavour by the Kuwait government to eulogise and indeed preserve the behavioural culture surrounding pearl diving.

A third area for investigation was that of forms of contemporary cultural expression. An interesting, possibly unique feature of Gulf culture is its ability to synthesise traditional and modern forms within the Gulf vernacular and then to project them into the Arab world beyond, by means of the vast media resources based in the Gulf. Poetry, long a medium of personal, social and political expression in the Gulf, is an excellent case in point. The runaway success of Poet of Millions, a television programme in which poet contestants utilise traditional poetic forms to address contemporary issues, exemplifies this synthesis and its spreading appeal. The more conservative presentations by Gulf performing artists have contributed to their popularity in an increasingly religious Arab world. Nimah Nawwab's poetry and reflections on it in this volume provide illustrations of the rapid evolution of this form of expression and its application to even quite sensitive personal, social and political issues. The incredible popularity of football in all GCC states, its centrality to cultural expression and its utility in forging strong national cultural identities, are themes explored by Abdullah Baabood. Nada Mourtada-Sabbah and her co-authors focus explicitly on the role of the media, in the form of both programmes and advertisements, in projecting a globalised culture within a Gulf vernacular. They conclude that despite the use of that stylistic vernacular, global norms and ethics promoted by the media are rapidly eroding what remains of traditional lifestyles and beliefs.

The implications of rapidly changing popular culture in the region for political cohesion, identity and authority provided the final area of investigation. As just mentioned, Gulf states are seeking to assert their sovereign lineages and the collective identities of their native citizens through support for a wide range of cultural-heritage preservation activities. But the relationship between state and society, between politics and culture, is not just a top-down one. Political systems and states are also shaped by cultural forces welling up within society. Indeed, cultural change can take on ominous, threatening tones for established political orders. Christopher Davidson takes up this theme in his investigation of how different rates and types of economic change in two emirates within the UAE illustrate the risks of possibly overly rapid change. His prognosis is that Dubai, globalising at a faster pace than anywhere else in the Gulf or possibly the world, will confront the issue of cultural anomy and even the disaffection of its native population. By contrast, Amr Hamzawy emphasises a pattern of state-society accommodation that is long established in the region. Despite rapid sociocultural and economic change, including growing heterogeneity of Gulf populations and an accompanying tendency to perceive and act upon particular interests, established political frameworks are not, in his view, under serious threat. Ruling families and the states that they, along with their populations, have constructed, are accorded legitimacy and acceptance within the context of a state-society bargain that allows for a steady expansion of public space. The rapid evolution of Gulf culture, obviously shaped but not determined by state policies, attests to the fact that those policies are not intended to thwart cultural expression or change.

Lubna al-Kazi's concluding demographic profile of the GCC states reveals societies in different stages of transition, as is exemplified most dramatically by gender differences in such areas as education and political participation.

The topic of this conference and the volume based on it are of relevance not just to citizens of the Gulf. While they have a clear interest in broadcasting to the world the distinctiveness of their culture and the state sovereignty grounded upon it, they are not just fabricating a story, as this volume attests. The transition from tradition to modernity in the Gulf is particularly interesting precisely because it is so recent, so profound and so rapid. Moreover, the cultural and political models they are projecting are virtually unique. As regards culture, no region of the globe is so simultaneously localised and globalised, so rooted in unique traditions and yet so interactive with the world. While some might call this cultural schizophrenia, others see a remarkable ability to synthesise and create a distinctive, adaptable and productive culture. At the political level the very fact that all six of the GCC states are monarchies provides formal evidence of the region's political uniqueness. While a generation ago scholars were forecasting the end of monarchies in the world and in the Gulf, more recent interpretations have come to appreciate the political strengths of this form of government and are now predicting its longevity. What is particularly interesting is that this most traditional form of government, consigned a generation ago to the dustbins of history by political scientists, is now presiding over extremely rapid social change which it is accommodating through a faster expansion of political space than are Arab republics.

In conclusion, this volume is intended to inform readers about Gulf culture, how it is evolving and with what political consequences. All of us involved in its production are hoping that it helps to overcome pervasive and misleading stereotypes, while simultaneously contributing to our understanding of extremely rapid sociocultural change and its political impact.

ONE

Heritage and Cultural Nationalism in the United Arab Emirates

Fred H. Lawson and Hasan M. al-Naboodah

Cosmopolitanism enjoys a long and vibrant history in the communities situated along the southeastern shore of the Gulf. Close commercial and religious contacts with Iran, central Arabia, the Indian subcontinent, east Africa and southeast Asia created a rich and complex *mélange* of cultural idioms and practices in the territories that made up the early twentieth-century Trucial Coast. Cultural pluralism remained a characteristic feature of local society during the years immediately after the formation of the United Arab Emirates (UAE) in December 1971. As oil revenues flooded into the country over the next two decades, however, indigenous components of popular culture steadily diminished. On one hand, *nouveaux riches* citizens abandoned established ways of life and adopted more attributes of the industrial world. On the other, the oil boom attracted large numbers of expatriate labourers, who brought with them the icons and mores of their respective homelands. By the early 1990s, popular culture in the UAE consisted almost entirely of idioms, symbols and practices that originated outside the country.

Faced with these trends, a number of influential actors took steps to encourage greater public awareness and appreciation of older forms of cultural expression. Senior members of the UAE's ruling families sponsored the formation of a network of clubs and agencies to promote respect for the country's heritage (*turath*). Such organisations included the Emirates Heritage Club in Abu Dhabi, the Folk Arts Society in Dubai, the Heritage Directorate in Sharjah, the Documentation and Studies Centre in Ras al-Khaimah and the Fujairah Cultural Organisation.[1] These bodies began to host lectures, seminars, book fairs, exhibitions and festivals to preserve and celebrate the rapidly receding cultural traditions of the pre-oil era.

As a complement to the network of heritage societies, a cluster of more specialised centres was inaugurated as the 1990s drew to a close. Among these was the Sheikh Mohammed bin Rashid al-Maktum Centre for Cultural Understanding, which opened in Dubai in March 1999. It took upon itself the task of 'familiarising expatriates with various facets of local culture', and announced that it intended to 'conduct familiarisation and Arabic language courses as well as lectures on Islam, in addition to guided tours of local homes and places of worship'. At the same time, the Zayed Centre for Heritage and History opened in al-'Ain, under the patronage of the UAE's deputy prime minister and president of the Emirates Heritage Club, Sheikh Sultan bin Zayed Al Nahayan, to promote scholarly research on the traditions of the Arab Gulf states in general and the UAE in particular.[2] It announced plans to publish a series of books, pamphlets and brochures; to forge links with overseas universities and institutes; to confer an annual award for *turath* studies; and to set up an archive and library containing relevant documents, reference materials, monographs and academic journals.

The Zayed Centre immediately initiated an Oral History Project to create a permanent record of daily life in the emirates in the years before oil. The interviews that were conducted as part of the project were deliberately carried out in an unstructured fashion, so as to allow the elders of the community to narrate their recollections in whatever way they thought best. Some told stories of momentous events that they had witnessed or in which they had played an active part; others described the everyday struggles and hardships that they had endured. Still others took the opportunity to recite poetry composed to commemorate a notable occurrence or to express deep-seated emotions.

The Oral History Project has been carried out in three successive stages. First, the centre's staff gathered up and duplicated all recorded interviews that had been conducted in the UAE by specialists in folklore during the 1970s and 1980s. Around 400 such interviews have so far been preserved, which make up a significant archive, since most if not all of the interviewees are now deceased. Secondly, thirty-eight elderly people of special interest were interviewed between 1999 and 2003. Thirdly, interviews were carried out during the course of 2004–05 with more than 100 long-time residents of the oasis community of al-'Ain. Although many of the tapes in the Zayed Centre's archives have now been transcribed and indexed according to topic, much of the recorded material remains in raw form, awaiting further study and analysis.

One of the oral histories is a lengthy interview with Saif al-Riyami, a retired major general in the UAE armed forces. Al-Riyami served with the Trucial Oman Scouts from 1958 to 1966 and then joined the Abu Dhabi Defence Force after it was established in 1966. With regard to economic life in the past, he relates that many people's livelihoods depended on collecting and selling dried wood for sale in the market, and this is how people managed to buy the food and clothing they needed for their families. Farmers cultivated date palms and raised a variety of different livestock, especially oxen. A favourite way to spend leisure time was to gather in front of the mosque after evening prayer, to exchange news and to converse while sitting on small mounds called *araqeeb*. People often slept outside their homes in the open air, a form of repose often referred to as *al-siheeh* (healthy).

Another revealing interview preserves the recollections of Khamees al-Mirri, who is said to have been 120 years old. He worked early in life as a pearl diver, and then became a camel breeder. He notes that even though large numbers of people earned their living from pearl diving in the 1940s and 1950s, it was camel herding and the hunting of hares and other wild animals that enabled people to survive the winter. In addition, the slave trade continued to be a thriving business, and slaves were brought regularly to the oasis of Buraimi for sale to buyers based in neighbouring Saudi Arabia.

Sultan al-Darmaki's memories of al-'Ain date back to 1967, when he studied at the Nahayaniyyah school. The school was located near the current Clock Tower roundabout and was constructed of mud brick and plaster; it had only a few tables and desks. The roads of the town consisted for the most part of unpaved sand tracks at this time, and houses were built out of mud brick and date-palm leaves (*'arish*). There were very few cars. Most of the local population lived in al-Mu'tarid, al-Muweeji, al-Jimi, al-Qattara and al-Hili, because there were date-palm groves in those districts. Several canals (*falaj*), such as al-Da'udi, al-'Ain, al-Hili, al-Mu'tarid, al-Qattara and al-Jimi, supplied water to the fields and date-palm gardens. The old market (*suq*), where rice, bread and dates were sold from shops made of mud brick, stood close to the current premises of the al-'Ain Co-operative Society. A cement and brick factory was the first industrial plant in the town; electricity began to be supplied in 1968. The currency in use was the Indian rupee, which was followed by the Bahraini dinar and then, after the establishment of the federation, the UAE dirham.

Most of the oral histories depict the pre-oil era as a time of hard-won contentment. 'Akeeda al-Miheeri observes that life was strenuous, yet productive and fulfilling: farmers took care of the date palms in the summer, while wheat was grown and harvested in the winter. People from al-'Ain would travel to Abu Dhabi to sell dates and date-palm leaves. Others used to sell dried wood and charcoal. These activities provided families with sufficient income to get by. Saif al-Riyami concurs: 'Our times were beautiful, despite the simplicity of life and lack of money. People did not envy each other. Nowadays, hatred is everywhere. I remember how simple life was, despite the harsh and difficult living conditions.'

By collecting and memorialising such reminiscences, the Zayed

Centre has played a key role in formulating and codifying a notion of the heritage of the UAE that underscores the importance of the federation's more insular communities. Cultural icons, tropes and practices that merit respect by virtue of their connection to the past are found to have been concentrated in the agricultural and pastoral districts of the interior, whose inhabitants have predominantly been Arabic-speaking and Sunni, rather than in the polyglot cities of the coast. Furthermore, the image of the good old days that is presented in most interviews collected by the centre is one in which personal and collective self-sufficiency was not only possible, but in fact constituted the norm. Ties to the outside world appear to have been tangential to everyday life, and might well have been loosened or even severed with very little impact on the overall welfare of the community.

In addition to compiling an extensive archive of oral histories, the Zayed Centre has from the outset focused attention on the archaeology of the territories that merged to form the UAE. In April 2001, the centre hosted the First International Conference on Emirates Archaeology 'to examine the results of archaeological excavations and studies in the United Arab Emirates and to place these within a context of interaction with other cultures in the region', as well as 'to generate a greater awareness amongst academics and among the UAE population at large about the heritage and history of the country.' The conference programme included five papers on the late Stone Age, seven on the Bronze Age, six on the Iron Age, four on the late pre-Islamic period and six on the Islamic era.

Two years later, the centre organised the first annual symposium on archaeological discoveries in the emirates. Ahmed Hilal of the National Museum of Ras al-Khaimah reported on excavations carried out at a group of Neolithic tombs scattered around Qarn al-Harf, in the western foothills of the Hajar mountains.[3] Anne Benoist of the French Archaeological Mission in the UAE surveyed a major site near the village of Bithnah in Fujairah, observing that 'the aim of this research is to study the organisation of the landscape during the Iron Age period, and to compare it with other Iron Age settlement areas in other parts of the Oman peninsula'.[4] She concluded that, in the case of one particular grouping of three buildings and nearby altar at Bithnah-44, 'no similar site has been identified elsewhere in the region.'[5] In both cases, the distinctive character of the respective emirates was found to be reflected, or perhaps better presaged, in the archaeological record.

Christian Velde, also of Ras al-Khaimah's National Museum, summarised excavations and restoration efforts that had been undertaken at the fort at Falayah, the summer residence of the emirate's ruling family and the place where a pivotal treaty was signed in January 1820, which established British control along the southeastern shore of the Gulf. Velde remarked that 'in 1999 Sheikh Sultan bin Saqr al-Qasimi, director of the Department of Antiquities and Museums, Ras al-Khaimah, decided to restore this important historical complex and open it to the public.'[6] The stone fort at the site was built in the mid-eighteenth century, and exhibits 'the typical features of a fortified farmstead, with a palm garden, scattered houses, a tower linked to the main building and stone walls surrounding a large courtyard, which in times of danger would serve as a retreat for people and animals of the whole area and as [a] defence against any raiders.'[7] Included in the complex was an enclosed date press of a distinctive type, 'being designed in a leaf-shape with four finger-like, radiating channels rather than the rectangular date-press constructions used elsewhere.'[8] Michele Ziolkowski and 'Abdullah Suhail al-Sharqi described the architecture of a similar building at al-Fara in Fujairah, and pointed to four other such 'house-tower' complexes located in the emirate.[9] Drawing on the work of D. Kennet, the authors suggest that the house-towers of Fujairah most likely served 'as a place of refuge [for] the local community' in times of natural disaster or external threat.[10]

Included on the programme of the 2003 symposium were two papers that discussed recent research into the palaeontology of the UAE. Although one might not at first equate palaeontological findings with archaeological ones, the editors of the conference proceedings pointed out that 'the conservation of the UAE's archaeological heritage and its palaeontological heritage are intimately connected. ... Moreover, the process of educating the country's residents about the discoveries applies equally to both archaeology and palaeontology.'[11] In fact, the editors continue, 'previous work undertaken by palaeontologists from London's Natural History Museum and Yale University showed that Western Abu Dhabi's Late Miocene fossil fauna is of international significance, and the latest discoveries indicate that there is much more work to be done in this field.'

At the second annual symposium, held in April 2004, presentations dealt with Neolithic settlements at al-'Ain, Marawah island and Jabal al-Buhais; Bronze Age sites in Dubai, Sharjah and Ras al-Khaimah; and Islamic era complexes in Fujairah, Ras al-Khaimah and the western islands of Abu Dhabi. On the whole, the papers highlighted the distinctive features of local structures and artefacts, while making few if any comparisons to similar structures and artifacts that had been unearthed in neighbouring countries.

Besides oral history and archaeology, the Zayed Centre has from the beginning recognised the importance of encouraging greater public awareness of the urban heritage of the UAE. Three staff members were initially assigned responsibility to carry out research on the country's 'urban heritage areas', 'in order to increase their usefulness as well as the national identity of the state.' This component of the centre's overall mission is articulated in one of its first publications: *Urban Conservation Concepts for the New Millennium in the United Arab Emirates* by Professor Ahmed Salah Ouf.[12] The book opens with a brief summary of the urban history of the emirates that emphasises strategic and military aspects of pre-modern urban design. It then describes the government of Sharjah's efforts to restore the historic market district of al-Maraijah and the adjacent fort of al-Hisn. Both projects, Ouf points out, were aimed at bringing key historic structures back 'to their 1950s appearance. The decision was taken by the restorers and the historic area administrators,' he continues, 'as they were convinced that the 1950s held the best traditional shape of the buildings, even though information was available about the appearance of the building[s] at earlier dates.'[13]

In order to carry out the actual restoration of the two structures, 'in rural areas of the emirates and surrounding countries some of the craftsmen [who had been active in the 1950s] were actually located and asked about some technicalities of the process.' Older techniques were then 'documented and taught to a whole new generation of craftsmen and building masters, so that they can restore and rebuild [other structures] using the same traditional techniques.'[14] Unfortunately, a major problem quickly arose: the newly trained workers turned out to be 'all expatriates with a high turnover cycle, which makes it necessary to [supervise] the transfer of exact detailed knowledge about their crafts.' Furthermore, even after the restoration of several historic buildings around al-Maraijah had been finished, the district remained cut off from the active waterfront, disconnected from the city's current traffic network and oriented towards tourism rather than everyday commercial and financial activities. Ouf therefore advises that future urban conservation projects incorporate a clear 'sense of place' that is 'enjoyable' and 'has a strong heritage connotation, even if it might have never existed in the original city fabric.'[15]

In all of these ways, the activities of the Zayed Centre are laying the foundation for a significant shift in the cultural nationalism of the UAE. More precisely, the scholarship that has been sponsored by the centre constitutes a notable instance of what Miroslav Hroch calls Phase A in the development of nationalist movements,[16] the moment at which 'an original small circle of intellectuals rediscovers the national culture and past and formulates [or in this particular case refines] the idea of the nation.'[17] During Phase A of the nationalist project, dedicated students – professionals and amateurs alike – engage in 'a bewildering variety of practices and endeavours: the compiling of dictionaries and grammars, the erection of commemorative monuments, the establishment of newspapers and university chairs, the edition of ancient documents (legal, historical or literary), the writing of historical novels or patriotic verse, the composition of national music, the organisation of sporting events and the opening of museums and reading rooms.'[18] Such initiatives make up what Joep Leerssen calls 'the cultivation of culture. By that phrase,' Leerssen explains, 'I understand specifically the new interest in demotic, vernacular, non-classical culture, and the intellectual investment that takes such vernacular culture, not merely as a set of trivial or banal pastimes, or as picturesque "manners and customs", but as something which is worthy of scholarly attention because it represents the very identity of the nation, its specificity amidst other nations.'[19]

For Leerssen, the cultivation of culture entails three analytically distinct operations, which tend to overlap with one another rather than following a strict temporal progression. The first, which he labels 'salvage', 'is content with mere inventorisation (of language, discourse, artefacts or practices).'[20] Cultural salvaging takes a number of forms: 'Manuscripts are seen as the surviving vestiges of a pre-Gutenberg world implicated in a long process of attrition, dispersal and loss; oral poetry is stereotypically snatched from the lips of aging folk who have long memories but little remaining life expectancy; folktales and folk music are invariably part of a lifestyle which is threatened by modernisation' and so on.[21] The second operation, 'fresh productivity', involves 'the emergence of contemporary initiatives inspired by these historicist inventories and remembrances.'[22] It is most often reflected in 'the establishment of national museums and the restoration of ancient buildings', as well as in the revival of 'traditional sports and pastimes, or even traditional dress' on the part of 'clubs and associations' devoted to the promotion of folklore.[23] Thirdly, the cultivation of culture is bound up with 'propagandist proclamation', as nationalist activists draw on historically rooted icons and rituals 'to suffuse the public sphere with a sense of collective national identity.'[24]

Leerssen proposes that these three types of cultural cultivation can be accomplished in two quite different ways. One way is through the operation of 'social ambience', that is, 'by initiatives on the ground, often as part of an urban middle-class sociability most strongly represented among the professional classes, and involves the establishment of associations, city academies, book rooms, reading societies and clubs, and the establishment of newspapers or periodicals.' The other way is 'top-down, initiated, funded and/or overseen by the authorities, and involves the establishment and management of state-controlled institutions such as archives, libraries, universities or university institutes, national academies, museums or galleries.'[25] The trick is to investigate concrete cases to see which types of cultural cultivation take place through which mechanisms, and in what order. Different countries will almost certainly exhibit divergent patterns.

In the contemporary UAE, government-sponsored institutions have taken notable steps to salvage the few remaining vestiges of the rural culture that characterised the pre-oil era. Idioms and practices associated with the largely homogeneous, self-sufficient, agricultural communities of the interior predominate in the oral histories that have been collected and memorialised by the Zayed Centre. At the same time, the UAE's long history as a well-established community, with only marginal connections to the outside world, has been confirmed by extensive archaeological research. These notions stand at odds with the cosmopolitan, ethnically and religiously heterogeneous cultures that one finds in the coastal cities, particularly in the rapidly globalising city-state of Dubai. Trends in that particular metropolis have taken a sharply divergent trajectory from developments in less prosperous Sharjah, where projects that epitomise the fresh productivity of local culture have been most pronounced.[26]

Leerssen insists that the model he proposes is applicable only to Europe. He asserts that 'the type of cultural nationalism inventorised here is specifically European in scope. Its various underlying factors affected all of Europe, and hardly any non-European areas.'[27] Nevertheless, one of the most counter-intuitive elements of his analytical framework has played a central role in the cultivation of culture in the contemporary UAE. The salvaging of local icons and pre-oil practices has occurred in the context of 'territorially a-specific' interactions among a large number of like-minded scholars and intellectuals,[28] most notably the regular international conferences and symposia on both oral history and archaeology that have been sponsored by the Zayed

Centre over the past eight years. Just as in nineteenth-century Europe, dozens of individuals concerned with collecting and preserving the literature, music and folklore of their respective localities have come together at these events to exchange ideas. Consequently, anyone who wishes to analyse the dynamics of cultural nationalism in the UAE should 'not tether a given national movement to its "proper" country, or to the socioeconomic circumstances and conditions of that [specific] place, but must also situate developments in a dense and tight network of mutual contact and inspiration' that transcends state boundaries.[29]

Whether components of the more insular, self-sufficient, homogeneous national culture that is being cultivated by scholarship carried out under the auspices of the Zayed Centre will end up being propagated in any sort of concerted manner remains an open question. Two recent developments indicate that they may well be gaining strength. First, there has been a noticeable shift in the imagery that one finds on postage stamps issued by the federal government. In the two decades from 1973 to 1992, the UAE issued some 405 definitive and commemorative stamps. The great majority of these displayed pictures depicting the country's modernity, such as oil refineries, satellite communications stations and jet aircraft; portraits of the seven rulers and their palaces; the armed forces; and the ubiquitous stylised falcon. Others celebrated national festivals, such as Traffic Week (1973, 1976, 1981), Tidy Week (an anti-litter campaign, 1985), Municipalities and Environment Week (1987) and Arab Palm Tree and Dates Day (1987); national milestones, like the tenth anniversary of the United Arab Shipping Company (1986) and the tenth anniversary of the UAE University (1987); anniversaries of major international events, like the twenty-fifth anniversary of the United Nations Declaration on Human Rights (1973), the International Year of Disabled Persons (1981), the International Year of Shelter for the Homeless (1987) and the World Cup football championships in Italy (1990). Only nine stamps boasted images that illustrated the country's heritage. Two were issued in November 1988 to mark the first anniversary of the opening the National Museum of Ras al-Khaimah; one of these displayed a golden crown and the other a vase. Two more appeared in December 1989 to celebrate 'the revival of heritage'; both of these pictured a wooden sailing ship and a manuscript page from the writings of the fifteenth-century navigator Bin Majid. Then, in October 1992, five stamps were issued that depicted 'traditional musical instruments'. Thus only about 2 percent of the stamps that were issued during these ten years featured images of the UAE's national traditions.

In the decade from 1993 to 2002, the federal government issued 299 postage stamps. At least twenty-five of these displayed some aspect of the country's cultural heritage. Archaeological discoveries made up sixteen of them (four generic [1993], four from al-Qusais in Dubai [1994], four from Mulaiha in Sharjah [1995] and four from Fujairah [1996]); the cultural heritage of Sharjah was honoured on five (1996, 1997); and traditional handicrafts were illustrated on four (1999). Icons of the UAE's national heritage can therefore be found on more than 8 percent of the stamps that were issued in these ten years. From 2003 to 2005, another 199 stamps were released. Four show archaeological artifacts housed in the National Museum at al-'Ain (2003); four depict 'traditional homes' (2003); six illustrate 'traditional fashions' (2004); and five display old-fashioned pearl-diving implements (2005). During this three-year period, the federal government placed images that celebrate the cultural heritage of the country on almost 10 percent of the postage stamps it introduced into circulation, a remarkable jump from the decades immediately after independence.

Second, the authorities in Abu Dhabi, still the largest and richest of the seven emirates, have made a notable move in the direction of rationalising the institutional mechanisms through which official sponsorship of cultural heritage activities will be implemented from now on. In October 2005, the government of the emirate set up the Abu Dhabi Authority for Culture and Heritage (ADACH), and charged it with 'supporting and unifying the activities of the entities and institutions concerned with culture and heritage in Abu Dhabi'.

The new agency assumed the task of managing a wide range of cultural efforts: 'education, media, promotion of literature and arts, encouragement of artistic creativity, safeguarding cultural assets, development of museums, promotion of archaeological research, historical urban planning, management of cultural landscapes, conservation of the [country's] intangible heritage, as well as the development of cultural tourism.' Several existing heritage-related centres, including the National Library, the National Archives, the al-'Ain Museum and the Abu Dhabi Islands Archaeological Survey, were incorporated into ADACH.

ADACH quickly stepped up the campaign to collect and disseminate local heritage. The proceedings of the Zayed Centre's 2001 conference on the archaeology of the UAE were designated as a standard textbook for courses offered by the United Arab Emirates University at al-'Ain.[30] The purview of the National Archives was expanded to include various sorts of ethnological research. ADACH also signed a memorandum of understanding with Zayed University to promote the preservation and transmission of local heritage through education and the management of heritage resources. In 2006, the government-sponsored Centre for Documentation and Research signed a three-year agreement with Zayed University to expand the country's oral history archive. The director of the centre noted at the signing ceremony that 'the history of the UAE has not been [properly] presented. We are thinking of writing down the [oral] history of the UAE and integrating it as a subject at the primary and university levels.'

Perhaps more importantly, ADACH took over the operations of the Abu Dhabi Cultural Foundation, which had been set up in 1981 'with the aim of promoting culture, enriching intellectual thought, encouraging fine arts and highlighting the national, Arab and Islamic cultural heritage.' One major programme sponsored by the foundation has been the Arts Workshop, which offers early morning and evening classes in ceramics, drawing, calligraphy, sculpture and photography to the general public. With support from ADACH, such activities are to be augmented as a way to 'bring Emirati culture closer to the community through cultural performances, children's courses and displays of Emirati traditional crafts and gastronomy.' At the conclusion of a March 2007 folk poetry contest, Abu Dhabi's Crown Prince Sheikh Mohammed bin Zayed Al Nahayan emphasised the importance of exposing young people to the national heritage: 'As we nurture our young minds, age-old indigenous Arab traditions should be inculcated as this would help in moulding their identity.'[31]

Cultural nationalism is a dynamic feature of all modern societies. Crucial components of a national culture take shape as the nationalist movement begins to coalesce, but the precise mix of icons, tropes and practices that constitutes the national culture evolves over time. Joep Leerssen, following John Hutchinson, draws our 'attention to the iterative, recurring nature of cultural nationalism, its tendency to return again and again to its preoccupations.'[32] Indeed, he continues, 'in contrast to what the neat succession of letters A, B and C would suggest in [Miroslav] Hroch's phase model, the cultural agenda of nationalism does not cease when subsequent, more activist phases swing into action, but continues to feed and inform these.'

Research on heritage, oral history and archaeology that has been carried out under the auspices of the Zayed Centre has produced the rudiments of a significant transformation in the national culture of the contemporary UAE. Many of the idioms that have been cultivated through the meticulous work of scholars associated with the centre stand at odds not only with the globalising cosmopolitanism of Dubai but also with the rapidly diminishing ideal of the Bedouin,[33] a venerable icon that was intimately associated with the founding president of the UAE, Sheikh Zayed bin Sultan Al Nahayan. It remains to be seen whether the next generation of rulers across the federation embraces and propagates previously undervalued elements of the country's rich cultural repertoire.

Notes

1. Sayyid Hamid Hurreiz, *Folklore and Folklife in the United Arab Emirates*, London 2002.
2. Adnan K. Abdulla and Hasan M. al-Naboodah, eds *On the Folklore and Oral History of the United Arab Emirates and Arab Gulf Countries*, al-'Ain 2004.
3. Ahmed Hilal, 'Excavations at Qarn al-Harf 67, Ras al-Khaimah, 2001', in Peter Hellyer and Michele Ziolkowski, eds, *Emirates Heritage*, vol. 1, al-'Ain 2005.
4. Anne Benoist, 'Excavations at Bithna, Fujairah: First and Second Seasons', in Hellyer and Ziolkowski, eds, *Emirates Heritage*, vol. 1, p. 72.
5. Benoist, p. 85.
6. Christian Velde, 'The Residence of Falayah', in Hellyer and Ziolkowski, eds, *Emirates Heritage*, vol. 1, p. 89.
7. Velde, p. 95.
8. Velde, p. 96.
9. Michele Ziolkowski and 'Abdullah Suhail al-Sharqi, 'Bayt Sheikh Suhail bin Hamdan al-Sharqi, al-Fara, Fujairah, United Arab Emirates (preliminary study)', in Hellyer and Ziolkowski, eds, *Emirates Heritage*, vol. 1, p. 117.
10. Derek Kennet, *The Towers of Ras al-Khaimah*, Oxford 1995.
11. Peter Hellyer and Michele Ziolkowski, 'Introduction', in Hellyer and Ziolkowski, eds, *Emirates Heritage*, vol. 1, p. 4.
12. Ahmed M. Salah Ouf, *Urban Conservation Concepts for the New Millennium in the United Arab Emirates*, al-'Ain 2000.
13. Ouf, p. 34.
14. Ouf, p. 46.
15. Ouf, p. 99.
16. Miroslav Hroch, *Social Preconditions of National Revival in Europe*, New York 2000.
17. Anthony D. Smith, *Nationalism and Modernism*, London 1988, p. 56.
18. Joep Leerssen, 'Nationalism and the Cultivation of Culture', *Nations and Nationalism*, no. 12, October 2006, pp. 566–7.
19. Joep Leerssen, *The Cultivation of Culture: Towards a Definition of Romantic Nationalism in Europe*, Working Papers in European Studies no. 2, University of Amsterdam 2005, p. 22.
20. Leerssen, 'Nationalism and the Cultivation of Culture', p. 570.
21. Leerssen, *The Cultivation of Culture*, pp. 25–6.
22. Leerssen, *The Cultivation of Culture*, p. 26.
23. Leerssen, *The Cultivation of Culture*, p. 27.
24. Leerssen, 'Nationalism and the Cultivation of Culture', p. 571.
25. Leerssen, *The Cultivation of Culture*, p. 28.

26. Ouf, pp.40–52, John W. Fox, Nada Mourtada-Sabbah and Mohammed al-Mutawa, 'Heritage and Revivalism in Sharjah', in Fox, Mourtada-Sabbah and Al-Mutuwa, eds, *Globalisation and the Gulf*, London 2006.

27. Leerssen, *The Cultivation of Culture*, p. 31.

28. Leerssen, 'Nationalism and the Cultivation of Culture', p. 565.

29. Leerssen, *The Cultivation of Culture*, p. 17.

30. Daniel Potts, Hasan al Naboodah and Peter Hellyer, eds, *Archaeology of the United Arab Emirates*, London 2003.

31. www.uaeinteract.com, 22 March 2007.

32. Leerssen, *The Cultivation of Culture*, p. 12; John Hutchinson, *The Dynamics of Cultural Nationalism*, London 1987, pp. 40–6.

33. Donald P. Cole, 'Where Have the Bedouin Gone?' *Anthropological Quarterly*, vol. 76, Spring 2003.

TWO

Place and Space in the Memory of United Arab Emirates Elders

Nadia Rahman

In an effort to capture the pulse of the rapid changes in the United Arab Emirates, I conducted a series of interview with elderly citizens. The subjects of discussion reflect the various regions of the emirates and their lifestyles: the sea, agriculture, and their related vocations and cultures. It is also important to reflect on male and female experiences as this is a traditional society with clear gender roles and spatial boundaries.

The elders are proud of what they consider to be their generation's achievement: hard work, the discovery of oil and a generous national leadership. They are ambivalent, however, about buildings, cars and other trimmings of wealth as they view them as profoundly impacting their lifestyles. The elder generation's needs are simple and they resent the challenges and burdens of 'new structures' in their life. The places of their youth no longer exist. Simple buildings and houses have been demolished to build skyscrapers and cities. So, the tension is one of pride in development and wealth versus nostalgia for the past and the simple life. New vocations and physical infrastructure have altered society in the UAE in a few decades, taking with them the places that

house memory. The elders complain that materialism and consumerism have replaced production; thus a conservative society has been
replaced by an open one, where men and women come together to
make a living. The changes have especially affected women because
they used to work in the fields and in homes. What is disturbing to
some is that economic development is proceeding faster than they are
able to comprehend and absorb. Haj Khamis, a pearl diver, Haj Salem,
a dhow builder, Um Issa, a farmer, and Um Juma'a, a wife and mother,
are the elders with whom I spoke and whose stories I now report.

I

'There was nothing around here and along the Corniche of Abu
Dhabi. People lived in the *'arish,* which is a room made out of palm
branches,' Haj Khamis says. He is a seventy-five-year-old man from
Abu Dhabi, whom I met at the Heritage Club. As an active member,
he tries to contribute to preserving old stories of the emirates. He
recounts the way life was while he was growing up and how it all
changed. Insistent on the order in which the events took place and
the details that surrounded each event, Haj Khamis spoke about
how he had to become a diver after his father died, in order to help
support his family. 'We were just working hard in order to buy rice,
sugar, dates. There was not much else at that time,' he declares. 'Now
we go to these supermarkets and there are so many products that we
don't recognise that are brought from everywhere.'

'The sea is cruel and diving is hell.' He reflects on his diving days
with nostalgia and pain. 'Diving has no mercy – you can't rest and it
is very dangerous as you are forced to stay up to five minutes under
water without any diving equipment,' he says. Disoriented under
water, he used to think about his fiancée and the woman he loved,
for the period needed to gather the pearls. 'I used to see her in front
of me like a mermaid and she would occupy my mind in that brutal
environment,' he recalls. When he came up, he would discover at times

that he had been gathering stones instead of pearls.

'The seasons of diving varied but sometimes we would stay out at sea for three months so that we were able to pay our debts and have something left to live on. Every man waited for that day when we docked the ship and they got to see their families and count their fortunes. It was as if it was your wedding day again. No, no, more like you were reborn. It was brutal but pleasurable at the same time,' Haj Khamis explains. Of course, some men never came back and some came back with very little, which compounded their debts further for the following diving season. It was with great difficulty that they sustained their families. They looked forward to prospering better when they next ventured out to sea.

* * *

'Before petrol, men dived for a living. I never did, but I built ships for diving purposes,' says Haj Salem as he sits in his modest *majlis* in front of the shipbuilding workshop along the Abu Dhabi coastline, where his old friend Sheikh Zayed bin Nahayan used to visit him. When asked about his age, he says he is in his sixties but doesn't know the year in which he was born. At that time they did not keep track of these things, he says. His appearance suggests he is in his eighties. As a boy he worked as a day labourer at various workshops where he was needed. He learned to build ships from his father.

'The late president was very keen to keep this trade alive and pass it on to the next generation,' he says, softly avoiding any eye contact with the camera, a foreign object that he is nervous about. 'Sheikh Zayed, may Allah have mercy on him, used to come and visit me often. In fact he encouraged me to build this *majlis*, where we would gather. One day he asked me how many people I have and I told him that I have twenty-five employees. He looked at me and said, "Do you know that there are probably fifteen people who are depending on each worker's income for sustenance?" Haj Salem agreed with the late president but was not in a strong financial position to expand and hire more people. 'Sheikh Zayed understood my situation and told me that I should expand and hire another fifty people because the business must grow and the people must work together and prosper. He arranged for fifty workers to be assigned to me from the Ministry of Labour,' Haj Salem smiles. The late president was keen to push ahead with modernisation and development, but he was also committed to investing in keeping shipbuilding trades alive and making sure that they were passed on to the next generation. Although Haj Salem's children were educated and worked in the government and private sectors, he feels that he has taught many others this highly skilled and demanding craft.

* * *

Under the *abayah*, a bright green floral dress is visible at Um Issa's heels as she escorts me to the bullfight on a Friday afternoon in Fujairah. The sport is a vestige of the Portuguese presence. Her feisty smile cannot be hidden behind her *burqa*. 'Although the winner does not take home anything, I just love to come and watch,' she declares. While the women sit in air-conditioned cars watching from the windows, Um Issa stands alongside the men in the dusty field, pointing the various bulls out. 'I know these animals well, I used to breed them on my farm,' she says proudly.

Um Issa explains that when the British departed and a state was formed, the government gave a piece of land to every family. Land, she says, became a definition of her personal identity because it was her workplace. She worked the fields and raised animals and produced all types of fruits and vegetables. 'We used to have the nicest mangos, watermelon, tomatoes, pumpkins, olives. Now we go to the market and buy all these vegetables full of chemicals, which explain all the new diseases,' she explains. Um Issa complains about how people have abandoned agricultural work for office jobs, leaving the land to become saline and useless for farming. Although she raised seven children, she still managed all those years to tend to her animals and the fields. 'Most of the work outside was done before ten in the morning, before it got too hot. After that, it was work in the house, the cooking, the cleaning, the washing. It was all done by hand. No machines like now, but there was time to do everything,' Um Issa boasts.

The fifty-five-year-old Um Issa insisted that the Heritage Village in Fujairah, where she works from time to time, is a must-see to understand how life was then in comparison to how it is now. She spoke with great passion and longing for the way things were as she strolled along the courtyard of the makeshift village. 'I work here because it keeps me in touch with the way things were. I may be younger than the old generation, but that's the period to which I belong,' she explains. Each house is an *'arish*. 'This is the one room for everything: living room, dining room and bedroom. This is a gas lantern because there was no electricity. This is the *ja'aed*, which is basically a sheep's skin that we used to sit on. Here you have palm-tree weavings which we used as floor mats; two buckets connected with a piece of wood we used as a scale.' She points out the objects to her right and left in the small sandy room as her mobile phone rings. 'Hallo,' she quickly answers, and tells the caller she is busy doing an interview. 'You get used to these gadgets,' she says.

* * *

When I was led into Um Juma'a's house – she is a friend of Um Issa's – we found her weaving baskets in a small room, cluttered with coloured palm branches, to the side of a large luxury villa. At sixty-five, she insists on continuing to work on her handicrafts because she needs to continue to be productive. 'It's not because of need, blessings to Allah, but I cannot just stop working when I have done it all my life. You know, I still get very proud when someone buys the traditional pieces that I create. My eyes are not great these days, but look at the sequences I can arrange,' she boasts. To her, this small cluttered room is the most comfortable one in the house, where she feels she belongs. 'My children wonder why I leave this big house to sit in this room;

it's where I can drift into my life,' she says.

Um Juma'a led us to the women's *majlis*, which was nicely furnished with chairs all around. She placed a simple mat in the middle of the room, letting the beautifully decorated chairs sit idle behind us. Tea was brought; a few women relatives joined us. She was in her element. By entering the women's space in her home, she thought I was looking for the female secrets in her society. She proceeded to tell me that she was married at the age of nine and about the process of delivering babies at home in the old days. She nursed all the children whose mothers left them in her care, as they went to the fields to work. 'We had to help each other. Those who stayed behind looked after the children and I cannot bear to see children cry. I had many kids and I was always breastfeeding so when others were hungry, I just nursed them like my own,' she explains. 'Um Juma'a ended up breastfeeding all the children around and now they can't marry each other because they are brothers and sisters in nursing,' Um Issa jokes.

II

'We were not educated like this generation but we learned through socialising and listening to wise men,' Haj Khamis explains. As he walks on the desert sand with a camel in the background, Haj Khamis looks up and around him at the skyscrapers that define the capital, Abu Dhabi. Perplexed at the glass buildings and large villas that have replaced the original, humble dwellings of a few decades ago, he acknowledges the great achievements, but is still nostalgic for the simple life. 'There are some pearls I still have and never will sell. I keep them so that my children and grandchildren will understand my history and story. When they look at them, after I pass away, they will be reminded to say "God have mercy on him". I also keep them to remember the moments and the conversations, the faces and the smiles of triumph that surrounded the finding of each pearl,' he adds.

'There was no money but there was also no heartache either. There was peace of mind,' Haj Salem explains. 'There were no cars and now there are so many fast machines everywhere. You worry about your son getting into an accident. You worry about a lot of things.' He spoke at length about how unsettling cars were and how these foreign objects invaded his safe place. He looks back with fondness on a time when things were simple and clear and one understood the meaning of things and the function of every object. 'Things are moving so fast that one cannot understand most of what is going on,' he repeats.

'We led almost a communal life in the *'arishes*,' Um Issa explained, pointing to the old model homes with the courtyard in the middle. 'People were neighbours, and they lived together as one family. During *iftar* in Ramadan, each family would bring their food and sit and eat together. Of course, the men and women sat separately.' The women used to do everything. Now, she complains, maids do it all, and that is why modern women are always tired and inactive. 'I cannot stop working. I still have the farm and will not sell the land for development, but continue to work in it. It's my role,' she smiles.

Confined and disoriented in her big villa, Um Juma'a explains, 'We are hidden in these massive places with big fences which keep guests away. If you decide to go and visit your neighbour, the maid answers and says, "No one is home." In the old days, we used to just wave to each other and say "good morning", or just walk across and have some tea.'

Place is both the locus of events and a trigger for memory. That is what people hold on to so that they do not forget their roots. Part of the frustration is that old space is being destroyed and some- thing new is being created which is disconnected from the culture of these elders. While the elders are proud of what their generation has achieved in their country, they do not view the buildings, cars, and other trimmings of wealth as benefits that should alter their life to this degree. The only spaces that seem to come close to fulfilling a little connection to a place with which they identify are the ones they have created, such as the Heritage Club and villages, the remains of a shipyard, and the small rooms on the side of the large villas. These creations they consider to be of great importance to educate youths about their cultural antecedents.

In a survey of female university students in Dubai, which asked them how they viewed life during their grandparents' generation versus their own, the vast majority stated that they had great respect for their grandparents' achievements. Some complained, however, that during their lifetime there have been so many changes to the language that they do not fully understand even their grandparents' dialects, thus causing a rift in communication and in the attempt to learn more about life then. That noted, Emirati youths appreciate that life was more peaceful then, where couples could raise many children and create wealth by hard work alone. From the stories of the diving trips, to being married, to making their own fabrics, young women were attracted by that simple life. Strength, pride, respect, devotion and kindness are the words repeatedly used to describe the elder generation.

On the question of which are better days, now or then, there was a split. Some point out the gentler and kinder world of their elders in which people were closer and had a greater sense of security. Others highlight the easier lifestyle that they lead now, which is full of amenities, opportunities and prosperity, despite a change of values and more focus on the individual rather than the community. Young women complain that they are caught between modernity and technology on the one hand and tradition on the other. Although they are expected to be competitive, English-speaking, technologically advanced, modern professionals, they must also abide by traditional expectations. These, they explain, often collide. They are expected, for example, to lead socially conservative lifestyles, but find themselves after graduating in an international, gender-mixed environment where they have to adapt and perform. Some jobs also require that they work long and at times odd hours, something that they feel is frowned upon by their families and community.

Some of the values that youth in the UAE think they need in order to survive in a modern competitive global world are: productivity, commitment, hard work, competitiveness, resourcefulness, adaptability and pride. These are qualities that UAE elders possess. The commitment to preserve the place they inhabited is not only a testament to their contribution to it and to the history of the emirates, but it is also a guide to their grandchildren as they enter new and uncharted territory.

THREE

The Nationalisation of Culture:
Kuwait's Invention of a Pearl-Diving Heritage

Sulayman Khalaf

The ongoing process of inventing popular heritage culture in Kuwait, as well as in other neighbouring oil-rich Arab Gulf societies, is to be viewed as an aspect of nation building. As in the case of Kuwait, the production of popular heritage is directed at developing the ideological/cultural component of an emerging modern nation-state. In this chapter I will examine how the invention and reinvention of traditional popular culture, as manifested in the annual Pearl Diving Festival and the Kuwaiti Seaman's Day as living cultural museums, is being used to provide both cultural/symbolic material required for the making of the state, and also to generate support for the existing political authority structure.

New oil wealth, rapid social change, the collapse of traditional economies and modes of life and the wider enmeshment of the local oil economy and culture within the global economic-cultural system represent both empowerment and challenge to the process of nation building. The image of Kuwait, as an *'imagined community'* in Anderson's (1991) sense of the term, rests among other things on certain cultural, heritage-related foundations. These foundations are being produced and reproduced in the form of heritage institutions and cultural festivals that, in the final analysis, avail the Kuwaiti political community a constructed theatre, upon which such invented cultural themes are continuously promoted through modern media as national political culture. Cultural traditions become invented, old memories are invoked and traditional values and folklore are reaffirmed and celebrated by invoking nationalist patriotic themes and discourses. The production and celebration of popular heritage culture with particular poetic discourses and strategic essentialisms are aimed at safeguarding the particularities of the Kuwaiti culture and in turn their national political identity. This is particularly significant as global cultural forces and dynamics have been increasingly viewed as real and/or potential threats to the indigenous Kuwaiti traditional culture. Equally important, it enhances the image of national leaders and promotes the popular perception of their roles as both patrons-cum-guardians of national heritage as well as state modernisers.

The bulk of the ethnographic material for this chapter is based on fieldwork conducted in Kuwait about twenty years ago, when I accompanied divers on a pearling ship. This allowed me to observe the divers' work rhythm closely, photograph them in action and participate in their singing of pearling work songs. My interest in this topic of constructed Kuwaiti culture remained alive through personal communications with Kuwaiti and non-Kuwaiti informants in Kuwait. Also my intermittent follow-up research in Kuwaiti newspapers and television cultural programmes has helped in keeping me informed about these continuing festivals of Kuwaiti heritage culture, particularly after the Iraqi invasion of the country and its subsequent liberation in 1991.

The chapter has two major aims. First, it provides an ethnographic document describing the process of constructing/inventing Kuwaiti heritage culture occurring within the contexts of broader global processes that have resulted in major multiple transformations in the society. Specifically, the ethnographic focus will be on the annual Festival for the Commemoration of Pearl Diving, which for the last twenty-one years has taken place in the summer months of July and August. It was only interrupted for two years during the Iraqi occupation and its aftermath. Also I will look at the construction of the Kuwaiti Seaman's Day (*Youm al-Bahhar al-Kuwaiti*) as an interactive cultural museum along a stretch of seashore close to the heart of the old city of Kuwait. This was inaugurated on the country's twenty-fifth National Independence Day on 25 February 1986. The nomadic Bedouin way of life was also celebrated in 1986 in the Desert Day (*Youm al-Badiya*), situated on a large desert strip outside the town of Al Jahra, inhabited mostly by newly settled tribal Bedouin groups.

The second aim of this chapter is to analyse how the Kuwaiti oil-state orchestrates the construction of this heritage culture in the form of a living museum/theatre. As a cultural project, this invented museum culture is directed for the production of historic memories and nostalgia that becomes, in the very process of production, transformed through the state-controlled media machine into discourses of national politico-cultural representation.

Rapid Change

Generally speaking, the production of new cultural forms is only meaningful when we locate these forms within the broader context of societal transformations that shape not only people's lives but also their ideological outlook about themselves and the world they inhabit. Thus, in order to understand the process of inventing this traditional heritage culture and the political/cultural discourses generated within it, we need to look first at the rapid pace of change and the concomitant transformations that have occurred during the modern period of Kuwait's history.

From a politico-economic perspective, we can view the forces unleashed by the oil economy as primary determinants in giving particular forms and functions to a large number of socioeconomic, political and cultural institutions and trends in modern Kuwait. The advent of the oil economy has triggered in Kuwait, as well as in other oil-exporting Arab Gulf countries, a phenomenally rapid economic and sociocultural change. What one observer noted about contemporary life in Arab Gulf societies in general applies to Kuwait as well. 'The past is so recent in the Gulf that it has a real and a living effect on the present. There was no need for museums until a few years ago, as anything that might have been put on display was in daily use in people's homes or work place, and the point of museums is to show foreign cultures or past glories ... Now, all that is changing: the old ways are dying out, the memories are dimming, and the old men who knew it all are disappearing. The time has come to catch the fleeting past before it fades, so that museums are being founded, books are written and scenes painted.'[1]

The flow of oil wealth during the last six decades has brought about the collapse of economic activities such as pearling, seafaring, fishing, shipbuilding and small-scale oasis agriculture and nomadic pastoralism. The oil economy has brought about an unimagined overall prosperity for the Kuwaiti population, as it was literally transformed 'from rags to riches'. Subsequently, the entire society was propelled to adjust to an entirely new economic system that has become strongly integrated within the global capitalist system, as oil has always been a global commodity *par excellence*. The commercial sector in Kuwait, as in the whole Gulf region, has been modernised, and the old merchant families have been transformed into super-rich agents for multinational companies, selling consumer commodities and luxury goods. New capitalist economic conditions and lifestyles of high consumerism have been on the rise. The recent frenzy, since the mid-1990s, of building large numbers of ultra-modern malls represents air-conditioned dream heavens for Gulf shoppers, including Kuwaitis, who score very high on the scale of wealth and consumption in the whole region.

What emerged in Kuwait may be termed an oil mode of wealth distribution, generating an expanding welfare service economy which has been able, so far, to offer employment to a large majority of the population. In this mode, there is no particular social class that can lay claim to the ownership and control of the means of production and use the state, so to speak, to protect its class interests. Instead, we have a newly developing state structure, which controls the means of production and means of allocation of oil wealth in society.[2] Due to its basic enmeshment within the global market system, this oil mode lacks its own in-built dynamics, which can provide it with its own power and course of development. It remains subject to fluctuating global market conditions.

The main political transformations can be located in the following areas. The oil economy has bought about profound changes in the support structure of the sheikhly ruling family. Through their high offices in the government executive apparatus, the sheikhs have found themselves in direct control of the society's oil wealth. This freed the ruling Al Sabbah family from its old pre-oil financial reliance on the wealthy merchant families. It has also helped the rulers to come closer to the masses in society through building an extensive welfare system that reflected a new paternalistic, humane and caring image of the state. The modernisation of Kuwait has meant the building of modern institutional infrastructures through which wealth and welfare services have begun to flow among the population. In a para-doxical way, perhaps, this sheikhly control of oil wealth without resort to indigenous classes or pressure groups has pushed the state executive structure to be disarticulated in economic terms from society at large. This has given the oil '*rentier* state' in Kuwait and the larger Gulf a particular power configuration, thus enabling it to extend its domi-nation in unparalleled ways over the economy, society and culture.[3] What is very particular about Kuwait as a modernising traditional state lies in the fact that it has fused within its internal make-up what Marxist sociologists term the '*infrastructure*' and '*superstructure*' of the entire society. The Kuwaiti state has not only been administering the affairs of society but it has also been functioning as controller of means of production and means of allocation, thus shaping and controlling relations of production (employment) as well as ways and means of consumption in contemporary Kuwait.[4] The Kuwaiti state has become the largest and most powerful employer in society, with a bureaucracy that functions as the state's welfare strategy for distributing wealth. In the process, it exercises direct and indirect hegemony over its population, including the expatriate multi-ethnic groups. All these functions combined have given the Kuwaiti state an immense power of patronage and control extending over the activities of both political and civil societies. It is indeed this new power of patronage that is of interest to our purpose here, since the state has emerged as the patron and supervisor who orchestrates the production/invention of heritage culture as an aspect related to the making of its ideological identity.

With regard to sociocultural transformations, Kuwait has very rapidly become a highly urbanised society with most of the population, nationals and expatriates, concentrated in Kuwait City only. Migrant workers representing over 100 different nationalities and ethnicities constitute over 60 percent of the population. Traditional social and cultural forms, such as the tribe, clan, lineage and old neighbourhoods (*fereejs*) are no longer the main organisation of economic, social/cultural life. Some of them, however, still carry weight in affecting perceptions and behaviour. It is within the contexts of this newly emerging social/cultural reality created by these multiple transformations described briefly above that the invention and reinvention of heritage culture in Kuwait become sociologically meaningful to us.

Theatre of Kuwaiti Seaman's Day (Youm al-Bahhar al-Kuwaiti)

During Kuwait's twenty-fifth National Independence Day celebrations in 1986, the state, through the Ministry of Information and Culture, reconstructed what has been named as '*Youm al-Bahhar al-Kuwaiti*' (Kuwaiti Seaman's Day) in which pre-oil life conditions in the old town of Kuwait were reconstructed and replayed on a large stretch of seashore close to the city centre. The make-believe re-enactment of old economic activities based on the sea, like shipbuilding, fishing, the return from pearling, women's rituals while waiting for the returning ships, women washing clothes in the sea, the little neighbourhood with its small mud houses, little shops, the water carrier, the donkeys, the traditional popular coffee shop, etc., were all displayed and performed in great detail. Actors, mostly retired seamen and pearl divers, were on the scene: some were mending large sails, others rehearsing the craft of shipbuilding, some making fishing nets. Shopkeepers sat in their little shops with their modest goods on a few shelves. Entertainment places were given names such as 'al-Bahhar al-Kuwaiti Juice Corner', 'al-Bahhar al-Kuwaiti Ice Cream' and 'al-Bahhar al-Kuwaiti Restaurant'. The old market was recreated, with thirty small shops selling miscellaneous items. An exhibition hall was filled with sea arts and crafts, primarily constructed from seashells. About thirty-five children's swings and play stalls were planted on the scene in a particular area decorated with flags. Seven old ships were positioned close to the beach, and children amused themselves by acting out being

1. Women singers perform on the grounds of the Seaman's Day

2. Visitors look at goods in a traditional shop

3. Reconstructed model of old Kuwait as part of the stage-set of the Kuwaiti Seaman's Day

4   Divers on their ship with their *nouhkada*, singing and clapping upon
returning to camp base

seamen. Kuwaiti flags, both the old pre-independence red flag and the
new one, fluttered everywhere on the scene and patriotic songs filled
the air. A manned broadcasting station was in charge of selecting the
songs and making announcements to the public.

Thousands of Kuwaitis have flocked to take themselves
into a journey in their recent past. Their experience in the
Kuwaiti Seaman's staged museum expresses itself in the form
of a historical telescoping, in which actors re-enact collec-
tively a mode of life that oil wealth has swiftly swept away, yet
remains alive in the memories of elders. This living museum
invites its Kuwaiti visitors to experience their past in actuality,
to imagine it and to reflect on it. This communal national
imagining is guided in graphic ways by all the sets they see
and walk through and participate in. The entire space is
often filled with nationalistic songs, coming from different

loudspeakers planted throughout the grounds of the seamen's living museum. The songs express the special bond between the Kuwaiti citizens and their Kuwait, the blessed, all-good and all-giving homeland. A sample of the song lyrics, selected from about twenty songs I collected, shows the nationalistic sub-themes that constitute both national imagining and celebration of Kuwait as one political community.[5]

Allah Ya Kuwait (Oh How Wonderful You Kuwait)

Oh how wonderful my homeland, Oh how wonderful you Kuwait
You are my mother and my home; I redeem you with my soul
May Allah protect you, in my heart I keep you
You are the vision in my eyes
Your protection is my duty and commitment
The banners of your beautiful wedding may be protected from all
   evil eyes,
Oh how wonderful you Kuwait, you are my mother and my home
No matter how far I go, my return is always a festive day
My heart dances with joy, what more does my heart want
On the 25th February you rejoice, and so do I
We have Jaber, the faithful Emir
And Saad, the Crown Prince, the big tender heart
How wonderful you are, oh Kuwait
My mother and my home you are

Say to Her (Kuwait)
(Lyrics by Sheikh Fahd al Ahmad Al Sabbah)

Say to her, say to her,
With our lives and possessions, we redeem her soil.
Say to her, say to her,
For her sake we live, and for her sake we will die,
No elsewhere there is love matching our love for her.

Say to her, say to her, and pray for her
May Allah protect her soil and keep safe her Emir
My gallant fellows are her people
Say to her, say to her we will redeem her soil

We Cultivated the Land

We people of Kuwait!! Yes, yes
We ploughed the land with our nails
We planted it with our loyalty and devotion
We watered it with our human love
Yes, yes, yes, yes, yes, yes,
Yes, we are the people of Kuwait.
Salutations to our Kuwait, we built the fortification of our glory.
With fortitude and determination
We protected the soil of our homeland. We live free, free
Yes, yes, we are the people of Kuwait

The Promise (Wa'd ... Wa'd)

We promise, we promise,
To her we give our promise
For us she may remain protected,
And to her we may remain faithful
We promise, we promise

Close Ranks Together (Takatafu)
(Lyrics by Sheikh Fahd al Ahmad Al Sabbah)

Oh people of this land
Together close your ranks, young and old
Stand together for our land
We are for Her for ever,
Under the glory of our Sheikh

Our Kuwait is our treasure and support
May Allah protect her,
Every one of us is ready to protect our soil
Together close your ranks
This is the home of gallantry
Our Sheikh with his people united
Oh our Sheikh! Symbol of glory
Oh People of this land
Together close your ranks

I Swear by Allah
(Lyrics by Sheikh Fahd al Ahmad Al Sabbah)

By Allah I swear oh Kuwait ... oh Kuwait.
And by the book of Allah I swear.
If I walked the world, and if I searched the world
Oh my homeland I will never find a place like you.
May Allah bless you, oh Kuwait, oh Kuwait, oh Kuwait.
You are the land of goodness and freedom.
You are the symbol of our unity,
You are our true homeland
Your identity is Arab,
Oh, my homeland, you strike deep in history
May Allah bless you, oh Kuwait, oh Kuwait.

The Time Has Come

Time has come
Oh, hear the clock is striking
Each and every one, his sleeves he rolled up
Ready we stand, command us, oh Kuwait!
For your glory we stand up, oh Kuwait,
It is you Kuwait, who commands,
It is to you we give our obedience.

The time has come,
Oh, hear the hour is striking.

Commemoration of Pearl Diving

It is *al-dashah* day, literally meaning, 'entering the sea day' (Monday, 7 August 1989).

Scene one: The hour is 7.30 AM. The morning sun is already warm. The old pearling ships are lulled gently by the glistening grey waters of the Gulf. There is a slow-paced movement from the beach to the twelve boats anchored a short distance away. Four lambs are tethered to metal pegs on the beach to be loaded later onto one of the boats. They will be slaughtered as part of the food provisions for the divers in their night encampment base during their twelve-day mission. Things appear to be moving the right way. Only minor things are being checked out by the newly recruited divers.

Scene two: About 200 men and women gather under a large canopy overlooking the calm seawater; men in snow white *dishdashas*

5. Veteran pearl divers check on the conditions of the ships

6. Young divers on their way to their pearling ships

(tunics), women covered in black *abayas* (gowns), children, photographers and other media reporters. People are looking at the boats. The morning breeze is softening a little in the rising heat. People are waiting for the formal ceremony to start, so they can then say goodbye to their young sailors and divers. Tables, microphones, cameras are all ready for the occasion.

Scene three: High-spirited singing of old sea songs engulfs the young shaven-headed recruits. About 100 of them sing, clap and dance in the large hall while waiting for the official inauguration of *al-dashah* in the sea. In their T-shirts and *wazras* (apron-like sailor's garments), they clap with deafening intensity. Some jump up, dance for about ten seconds, then quickly retreat to their place and melt away in the heat of sea rhythm and song. Sweating young sailors, songs, camaraderie, laughter, joy and video cameras crowd the hall. Older men known as *noukhadas* (skippers) join in and as they clap they send their young sailors through a higher emotional charge. The singing-clapping sea rituals last for about twenty minutes before everyone feels out of breath.

Scene four: The hour is around eight. The hall door opens. A hundred and twenty young divers and sailors come out of the hall trailing each other. Each is wearing his T-shirt, *wazra*, a skullcap, with his diving rope and metal weights carried on his shoulders, his diving nose-clip in a string around his neck, and his net basket for his diving catch. They stand in a 50-metre-long line facing the large shade canopy where the guests and officials are seated. Official speeches are to follow.

Scene five: Fathers, mothers and brothers look on, video cameras move about documenting the event which is to be inaugurated under the patronage of the Minister of Social Affairs and Labour, Sheikh Naser Mohammed Al Sabbah. The under-secretary in the ministry, Abdul Rahman al Mazroui is deputising for the minister. In a brief speech the ministry under-secretary notes that this event, which is 'reviving our heritage' on the grounds of the Kuwaiti Sea Sports Club comes as the realisation of the emir's wishes to revive and preserve Kuwait's sea heritage. It is also important for keeping alive the memories of our fathers and grandfathers, and significant for teaching our youth the arts and skills of the old sea pearl-diving life. Moreover, the revival contributes to installing in our sons the spirit of loyalty and commitment to their nation.

The speech that follows is given by an old *noukhada* who is the chairman of the Committee for Sea Heritage Revival and in charge of the organisation of this pearl diving expedition. He starts:

> Brothers, uncles and sons! Yesterday you came and saw your own sons labouring hard fixing their boats. Today, as we will embark to complete our pearl diving journey, we want your prayers and good wishes for good luck. It is a new experience for many of the divers and they indeed need our prayers for good omen. This young generation grew up in today's society of plenty and urban comfort. Our youth have forgotten what manual work is all about. They have begun to shun away from it. We are here to experience and remember the harsh life of

our fathers and grandfathers.

All this is made possible by the support and wise leadership of His Highness the Emir and His Faithful the Crown Prince. The aim is not to harvest pearls so that we can make a living out of them, but to teach our youth what sort of hard life our grandfathers struggled with. The main goal is to train our sons about the old sea life ways and its challenges and also to make them value the high morals our grandfathers upheld for the common good of their community. This experience will do away with social differences among our young sons as they have to work hard, shoulder to shoulder, as one team on their pearling ships. We want to teach them to bear hardships and stand in the face of sea dangers and challenges.

On behalf of all the people participating in this journey we extend our thanks and immense gratitude to the emir of our homeland and to his crown prince and our wise government. For the Ministry of Social Affairs and Labour we hold all appreciation and gratitude and in particular for His Excellency Abdul Rahman al-Mazrou'i for his tireless efforts and support to make the project of our Heritage Revival Committee a successful one.

Scene six: The ministry official dressed in his black thin gown is ushered to the standing line of young divers who have stood silently during the formalities of speeches. As he approaches the line he begins shaking hands with each one of the 120 trainees, of different ages from twelve to twenty-two years old. While the hand-shaking goes on, a voice on the microphone speaks loudly, praising the spirit of these young men and their trainers in this summer Pearl Diving Academy. He also lauds the toil and sacrifices of Kuwait's grandfathers who challenged the sea for survival. Again the emir and the state receive more salutes for their support for this wonderful day.

Scene seven: Mothers, fathers, relatives and friends move down to the beach to bid farewell to their young divers. A large crowd gathers

7. Government officials greets divers before sailing off

at the beach. The water lulls the ships gently, while the divers settle
themselves on their decks. The *athan*, call for prayer, comes echoing
across the beach. It is the traditional way of signalling the start of the
pearling trip. Once the *athan* 'Allahu akbar' (God is great) is over,
the young sailors begin raising the sails of their twelve ships, donated
for this cultural project by the emir himself. The morning wind is
gentle. As soon as the white sails become pregnant with the warm
wind, the ships move away slowly. Mothers, fathers and little sisters
begin waving. Others are busy videoing the scene. Five minutes pass;
the white sails become dots on the grey horizon moving away from
the city beach scene in search of pearls, or what divers used to call
'tears of the moon', beneath the water. Small motorboats move about
carrying television media men. They are going to follow the divers'
ships for a mile or two to document and later publicise the pearling
journey to the nation. A helicopter flies over the ships for a while as
a salute and gesture of moral support to the journey.

At the Pearling Camp near Khairan Resort

A large contingency of thirty-seven media men working for daily newspapers and television visit the divers' base camp near Khairan, about 80 kilometres away in the south of the country. Their mission is to provide media coverage of this Kuwaiti cultural experiment in inventing national history. I opt here to cite notes and captions from newspapers reporting on this event, as I believe the very writing style and language used by the journalists is part of national self-representation. It is a media discourse produced for the Kuwaiti public to boost their imagination as regards their history and identity.

> The pearling journey sailed away to our ancestors' homeland. In actual geographical terms the homeland it sailed to is a particular camp base near Khairan Sea Resort, south of Kuwait, where Kuwaiti rich elite families come to spend their weekends and holidays in total modern luxury. The seabeds around there are known to be rich with pearl oysters.
>
> The 120 young divers and another twenty-four additional skippers, supervisors and helpers arrived at the camp grounds that offered rather Spartan and basic accommodation. On a concrete surface facing the moored ships and the sea beyond, four large tents were pitched for living and sleeping, and another two were designated as a kitchen and storage space for food provisions to feed the divers for the eleven days of their sea adventure. The tents were almost empty, furnished only with mats to sit and sleep on. Very much in contrast to their neighbours holidaying only one kilometre away in the Khairan ultra-modern resort. The divers are supposed to relive the harsh work and life conditions their ancestors experienced not too long ago.[6]

Snippets are presented from Kuwaiti newspapers portraying the divers' work and the rhythm of life in the camp and at sea.

The work day began with singing by *al-nahham* (the traditional pearling ship singer). Before sunrise the young men were ready to sail to the pearling areas. This is what they do every morning to earn their meagre livelihood. The sea is full of hidden good things but is also full of dangers. In the style of the old days, our young men of Kuwait Sea Sports Club re-enacted the seamen's lives in the Fourth Festival for the Commemoration of Pearl Diving. They are renewing the hard way of life in the same spirit as that which possessed the old Kuwaiti seamen. Their spirit was longing for all the challenges that may face them. Their means are the ships, the sails and rowing oars. They all have forgotten about motorised fast boats and air conditioners.

The divers' ages range from ten to twenty-five years old. They all have been assigned to their ships and trained to abide by the *noukhada*'s instructions. Their light breakfast is only a few dates and their lunch is what Allah provides and is eaten while working at sea. When the sun gets in the middle of the sky one of them raises the call for midday prayer (*Allah Akbar*). Seconds later you see them all in one line praying behind their *noukhada*. Then they rest a little, perhaps snooze a little. After that they resume diving to bring up more pearl oysters. This work pattern continues until about half an hour before sunset when all ships sail back to the camp with the young divers all exhausted. Upon arrival they get busy tiding their ships, taking the oyster shells out and storing them in a large container. Later on in the evening they will open them up. They wait anxiously for their dinner as it is their main meal for the day. After dinner, *as samra* begins, the traditional night party filled with sea folklore songs, clapping and dancing.[7]

Another reporter in *Al-Watan* newspaper detailed his observations in a full page with thirteen documentary photographs.[8] 'Seven thousand oysters are the catch of the last three days.' 'Discipline, patience and the *ya mal* sea songs are the days of the pearl divers.' He then writes:

> All you can see in the divers' camp in Khairan speaks about
> hardship and scarcity. Even the air is scarce with breeze. We
> are in August and high humidity is there in abundance. When
> you look at the divers you see how the sun has darkened their
> skin. Their bodies look firm because of the hard work they
> perform. On their ships they dive, they pull ropes, they row,
> and they raise sails.
>
> In the camp everything runs according to strict order, con-
> trolled by the whistle of the chief supervisor, Hassan Rajab.
> The boys have become familiar to the calls of his whistle.
> The 7.30 whistle signals dinner time. The divers sit in circles
> around large food trays to have dinner in a communal way.
> Upon finishing, they take away the trays and tidy their tents.
> The supervisors are strict, yet they deal with the divers as if
> they are all members of one family. At night, their entertain-
> ment revives the old folklore of sea work: songs, drum music,
> clapping and dancing.
>
> It is dark in the distance; the camp is lit up with a small
> electricity generator. When the hour reaches ten, the whistle
> echoes through the camp. It is bedtime. No beds, only floor
> mats for everyone. The generator gets turned off. The camp
> goes to sleep early; it also rises early with the sunrise.

The pearling expedition lasted for twelve days. The closing day of the
journey is traditionally referred to as *youm al-qifal* and, like the start
of the expedition, this was a great occasion that put the state media
machine in Kuwait City in full gear. This documents and celebrates
the return of the divers and their trainers, who have revived for the
modern nation the heritage of its ancestors. With radio, television and
several dailies involved, mass media coverage was ensured – and subsequently everyone in the homeland was able to participate symbolically
in these state-orchestrated Kuwaiti sea heritage celebrations.

Analytical Discussion

Several analytical notes can be extrapolated from the ethnographic description presented above.

1) As noted earlier, the oil economy led to a total collapse of pearling as a traditional industry in Kuwait. Actually, prior to the advent of oil, this industry had already received serious blows as a result of the world depression in the 1930s and the introduction of Japanese cultured pearls in the world market before the Second World War. The old pearling ships and their folklore were folded away in school textbooks and recently built museums. However, Kuwait as an emerging nation-state armed with a huge financial capital surplus needed another equally important capital of a symbolic kind to give itself the necessary historical depth and cultural anchorage. The invention of its historical pearling traditions is intended to realise such a political/cultural goal. In this context, this invention process falls within what Lofgren calls 'the nationalisation of culture'.[9] According to Hobsbawm, 'invented tradition' means 'a set of practices, normally governed by

8. Pearling ships decorated with the old Kuwaiti Red Flag

9. Pearl divers on their ships in the sea

10. Panoramic view of pearling ships sailing back to camp before sunset

overtly or tacitly accepted rules and of a ritual or symbolic nature which seek to inculcate values and norms of behaviour by repetition, which automatically implies continuity with the past'.[10]

2) The historic past of Kuwait is near in temporal terms, yet the magnitude of socioeconomic transformations generated by the oil revolution has distanced it from people's everyday life and awareness. However, the fact remains that many of the elders in Kuwait span in their own personal lives the two modes of life, that is, pre-oil and post-oil. This made it easy for the state to reach out to those veteran divers (*al-ghasa*) and ship captains (*noukhadas*) and mobilise them to contribute their traditional knowledge and expertise for the production of this national cultural project of Kuwait, which has now taken on an institutionalised form since its inception in 1986.

The construction of this significant link with the nation's history was frequently vocalised by state officials, as well as the young divers who went through the pearling experience. Abdulla, a university student, said, 'Life in the past was harsh and difficult, but had a delightful flavour. I am proud of my grandfathers.' Ahmad, a sixteen-year-old student, said, 'Some of the divers felt that the journey was labour-intensive and tiring, and they expressed their wish to quit, but I enjoyed thinking of my grandfather who was a pearl diver.'[11]

3) The Kuwaiti state plays a primary role in the production of these invented traditions of the old pearl-diving culture. This is fully understandable in comparative terms, as the invention of traditions is basically about nationalism. Lofgren writes:

> The interesting paradox in the emergence of nationalism is that it is an international ideology that is imported for national ends. Looking back at the pioneer era of Western national culture-building we may view this ideology as a gigantic do-it-yourself kit. Gradually a set of ideas is developed as to what elements make up a proper nation, the ingredients which are needed to turn state formation into a national culture with a shared symbolic capital.[12]

It is relevant to note here that the official emblem of the state of Kuwait is a pearling ship embraced by the new post-independence Kuwaiti flag. The main state agencies involved in the production of this Kuwaiti annual cultural enterprise are the ruling emir, the Ministry of Culture and Information and the Ministry of Social Affairs and Labour. The symbolic gesture signifying the central role of the state is manifested at the end of the pearling expedition, when the harvested pearls are offered ceremonially as a gift to the emir who had donated the twelve ships for this cultural national project. In addition to the state's primary support, a sizeable number of private companies and businesses give additional contributions to the pearl diving commemoration festival. For example, in the fourth festival of 1989, thirty donors gave financial contributions, and their names were registered on many of the posters that were displayed, along with the names and photos of the 120 young pearl divers.

The state mobilised its media machine to give the event huge national media coverage. Both state and independent newspapers were there *en masse* to document the celebrations, with extensive displays of photos and journalistic discourses that revolved around the themes of national unity, quasi-romantic glorification of the harsh life and struggle the pearl divers and sailors endured in the past, and praise for the national leaders for producing these historical national festivals. The Kuwaiti sea pearling heritage (*turath al-ghuos*) has become appropriated by the state as a kind of state folklorism. The spin-offs from this cultural concern with pearling popular heritage have been reproduced over the last twenty years in a rather colourful national television culture. Every year during Kuwait's National Day (25 January), Kuwait's two most celebrated singers, Shadi al-Khaleej (Nightingale of the Gulf) and Sana al-Kharraz, appear in an operetta-like production, and lead hundreds of school boys and girls in festive performances of singing, dancing and re-enacting of the pearling culture. In the process they glorify Kuwait as a nation and a state. Those boys and girls receive extensive training to produce extravagant national heritage television shows. Usually the Emir of Kuwait, ministers and other government VIPs are present at these shows, which are also televised live throughout the nation. The systematic reproduction of this sea heritage culture in this media form contributes to the citizens' perception of Kuwait as an inclusive 'imagined community'. [13] It has also made national celebrities of the two singers. Shadi al-Khaleej has a great tenor-like voice and has been transformed through these celebrations into a super national star. Sana al-Kharraz was in the mid-1980s only a secondary school girl when she first started singing for the glory of her nation.

The state appropriation process of national heritage is not peculiar to Kuwait or other Gulf countries, but is also found in many European and Asian countries. In Eastern Europe folk peasant culture was created by state agencies as a national type contrasting with neighbouring countries. Now both the state and the tourist industry are chief agencies for the invention and reinvention of such stereotypes of national culture. [14] The Gulf countries offer numerous comparative examples about the importance of this newly constructed heritage culture in their rapidly changing societies, where the state is the patron and the organiser of this new/old culture. Camel racing, dhow racing, popular poetry (*nabati*), television programmes, heritage clubs, heritage research centres and heritage villages are among the most media-promoted heritage activities and sites. For example, the Janadiriyah, a celebratory cultural event in Saudi Arabia (named after a site outside Riyadh), is featured at length every year on television, sometimes featuring the king and other Saudi emirs doing the '*adrdha* sword dance with hundreds of dancers recruited from the National Guard for this event. The cultural discourse generated in these activities is geared towards maintaining the nation's sense of cultural authenticity (*asala*), celebrating the achievements of national leadership and safeguarding against the global culture, which is regarded by many as a generalised threat to the local cultural identity. [15]

4) At an implicit level, both the Kuwaiti Seaman's Day and the pearling celebrations as heritage constructs represent an image of 'limited good' encapsulated within the modern and affluent urban

setting of Kuwait City, where images of 'unlimited good' prevail.[16] The simulated traditional life stands as a surrealistic collage contrasting sharply with the wealth and comfort of present-day life and thus carries double images and meanings for the Kuwaitis. On one hand, it is a positive image as it helps the young to experience the economic and social life of their ancestors, and provides a useful historical link to the present. On the other hand, it is a negative image displaying 'days of poverty' (*ayyam al-faqr*).

Thousands of Kuwaitis flocked to take themselves into a journey in that museum of their recent past. It was evident from the reactions and comments of youth and adults that this journey into their constructed past was similar to going through an old family album. They try hard, as they gaze through the yellow pictures of the dead, to identify some impressions and outlines that may help them relate to their own present self and the world they now inhabit. Young men and women armed with video and snapshot cameras could hardly believe that drinking water was so scarce and was carried in black rubber bags on donkeys as shown in the rehearsed life setting, and that the homes of their fathers and grandfathers did not have electricity, refrigerators, radios, washing machines, televisions and other modern conveniences which are now taken for granted.[17]

The implicit messages generated in the minds of visitors and participating actors revolve around the idea, 'Let us all be thankful to Allah for his grace and be grateful for our caring welfare state and its rulers'. The signifiers of this political-cultural discourse can be identified through images of juxtaposed contrasts: the past versus the present, pearl diving versus the oil economy, image of 'limited good' versus image of 'unlimited good', harsh life versus comfortable life, donkeys versus cars, mud houses versus modern homes of concrete and glass, colonisation versus independence and freedom.

5) The streaming of nationalist songs across these festival spaces generates a nostalgic tribute to the images of the past, but, more importantly, they give greater celebration to the images of present-day Kuwait. As the singing voice hovers across this living heritage museum,

it subconsciously induces collective imagining and national loyalty to the motherland, as it is often referred to in these loud repeated songs.

The Seaman's Day, as an invented heritage display, celebrates a set of Kuwaiti cultural traditions and forges a new political language that is best expressed in the nationalistic poems and songs that are broadcast for four to five hours each evening. The patriotic national theme exalts the achievements of Kuwait's development as a modern nation-state. The nationalistic language and tone became much more intense when the entity of the state was seriously challenged by the Iraqi invasion in 1990 and its subsequent liberation in 1991. The songs, many of them written by the late Sheikh Fahd al Ahmad Al Sabbah, emanate from a fixed source: the radio broadcasting room (*al itha'a*) built on the stage set itself. The lyrics tell us about a utopian imagined vision of the contemporary Kuwaitis' political perception of themselves. This ritualised practice of reciting, broadcasting and singing folk poetry about Kuwait as emerging nation-state represents a sociopolitical act of constructing oneself as a member of a political community. Moreover, the songs as a political-cultural voice represent discourses of the state celebrating its own progress, and describing it as benevolent, caring and committed to the welfare of its people. In this lies a latent call for support and legitimatisation from its citizenry.

6) Content analysis of the song lyrics and the material display of old economic and cultural activities provide in both heritage settings a purpose-built theme of nostalgia. Nostalgia is a kind of currency: the more it circulates the greater its power for creating common bonds, perceptions and imagining. It is a significant component in invoking collective historical memory. The songs, the official speeches delivered on the inauguration day of the pearling fleet and the media coverage emphasise new ideological-cultural signifiers that are directed at community integration and nation-building. Thus, certain historical and/or present social and economic facts are deliberately absented or, better perhaps, mystified. There is no representation or mention of any real or possible areas of class or ethnic or religious tension, discord or disparities.

Yet, it is well documented by economic and social historians that class disparities were great and conflicts of class interest infested the traditional pearling industry. The poor divers always found themselves in debt bondage to the ship owners, who constituted a small but powerful merchant class.[18] Even folklore songs attest to this historical fact.[19]

> Oh God with my eyes I look at you
> Pay (for us) the debts we carry
> Pay (for us) our heavy debts
> The old debts and the new

When ships returned, women waited at the beach to receive their beloved ones. The songs they sang reflect the exploitation and harsh life the divers endured.

> Singer: Oh brothers! How pretty the sight of ships arriving at the beach.
>   Chorus: You are right
> Singer: Oh their captain, (please) do not be harsh with them
>   Chorus: You are right
> Singer: Our boys are still young, look how hard they pull their oars
>   Chorus: You are right
> Singer: Oh you their captains! Do not be harsh with them
>   Chorus: You are right
> Singer: Don't you see how the diving ropes have cut deep in their palms
>   Chorus: You are right
> Singer: Don't I wish I was butter to anoint their hands
>   Chorus: You are right[20]

7) Essentialising and mystifying the past community is a purposeful cultural strategy. The only mention of struggle relates to the old

imagined community struggling with the sea, harsh life and poverty. Conflicts of interests among groups, sects or classes in Kuwait's pearling old life are deliberately ignored. This appears to be a common and recurrent feature in invented traditions across cultures. It relates to what we may call political craft in the nationalisation process of heritage cultures in which state agents can manipulate and design invented cultural displays in particular ways with particular discourses, to achieve certain common ideological goals that are deemed essential for national identity building.

The stage sets presenting Kuwait pearling as an invented tradition are conveniently used by media specialists as arenas from which to lavish praise on the ruling family. When analysing the songs, poems and speeches and other graphic representations of the idealised image of the ruling sheikh, they appear to portray him at the same time as both the guardian of heritage and tradition and a state moderniser, whose wise vision helped in the rapid development and creation of a caring welfare society.

Concluding Remarks

In conclusion, Hobsbawm and his colleagues noted that 'the invention of traditions' is expected to occur more frequently when societies go through rapid transformations. This statement has been substantiated by numerous comparative studies on European and non-European societies during the last 200 years.[21] This observation applies as well to the Arab Gulf states, as construction of past heritage has reached levels of a national cultural industry. The scale of this newly produced heritage culture appears to be commensurate with the speed and scale of change these societies have experienced in their post-oil, globally driven, modern conditions.[22]

In the same vein, comparative studies by anthropologists and sociologists inform us that 'old societies' had to deal with the challenges of building 'new states' by resorting often to their popular folk culture to draw from for the building of unified imagined political communities with modern state national ideologies.[23] Kuwait's invention and reinvention of its sea pearl diving heritage illustrates this general statement rather well. Both the Pearl Diving Festival and the Seaman's Day are invented as theatres of Kuwaiti past culture, to provide not only historical continuity and anchorage to a rapidly changing society, but also support the very making of modern national identity. The constructed/invented pearl diving traditions in Kuwait illustrate the utilisation of national heritage (*al-turath al-Kuwaiti*) for forging a new politico-cultural identity for citizens. As a process, the annual reproduction of these cultural living museums helps the modern state to tap into history and tradition to build and reinforce its ideological dimension. New elements, themes, symbols and meanings are invented, synthesised and organised to produce new cultural forms that are linked to the historical past. These theatres have become institutionalised cultural living museums, operating within new socio-economic and political realities geared for serving the present and the future of the nation. They communicate new politico-cultural discourses to the contemporary Kuwaiti community. This ongoing cultural/political process, as evidenced in the Kuwaiti example, is found in similar patterns throughout the oil-rich Arab Gulf states.

Notes

1. John Bullock, *The Gulf: A Portrait of Kuwait, Qatar, Bahrain and the UAE*, London 1984, p. 139.
2. Jaqueline Ismail, *Kuwait: Social Change in Historical Perspective*, Syracuse 1982.
3. Giacomo Luciani, 'Allocation vs Production States: a Theoretical Framework', in H. Beblawi and G. Luciani, eds, *The Rentier State*, London 1987.
4. Sulayman Khalaf, 'Gulf Societies and the Image of Unlimited Good', *Dialectical Anthropology*, vol. 17, 1992, pp. 53–84.
5. Benedict Anderson, *Imagined Communities*, London 1991.
6. *Al Seyasah* daily, 8 August 1989, p 1.
7. *Al-Anba Al-Kuwaitiyya*, 8 August 1989, p. 2.

8.   *Al-Watan*, 13 August 1989, p. 9.

9.   Orvar Lofgren, 'The Nationalization of Culture', *Ethnologia Europaea*, vol. 19, 1989, p. 8.

10.   Eric Hobsbawm, 'Introduction: Inventing Traditions' in E. Hobsbawm and T. Ranger, eds, *The Invention of Tradition*, Cambridge 1997, p. 1.

11.   Reported in the *Al-Ittihad* newspaper, 12 September 1994, p. 21.

12.   Lofgren, p. 8.

13.   Anderson.

14.   Lofgren.

15.   Paul Dresch and James Piscatori, eds, *Monarchies and Nations: Globalization and Identity in the Arab States in the Gulf*, London 2005.

16.   Khalaf, 'Gulf Societies'.

17.   Khalaf, 'Gulf Societies'.

18.   Mohammad Al Rumaihi, *Obstacles of Social and Economic Development in Contemporary Arab Gulf Societies* (in Arabic), Kuwait 1977.

19.   Hissa Al-Refa'i, *Songs of the Sea: A Study in Folklore* (in Arabic), Kuwait 1985.

20.   Al-Refa'i, p. 321.

21.   Hobsbawn.

22.   Sulayman Khalaf, 'Poetics and Politics of Newly Invented Traditions in the Gulf: Camel Racing in the United Arab Emirates', *Ethnology*, vol. 39, no. 3, Summer 2000, pp. 243–61 and Sulayman Khalaf, 'Globalization and Heritage Revival in the Gulf: An Anthropological Look at Dubai Heritage Village', *Journal of Social Sciences*, vol. 19, no. 75, Fall 2002, pp. 277–306.

23.   Clifford Geertz, ed., *Old Societies and New States*, New York 1963.

FOUR

An Aspect of Cultural Development in Bahrain: Archaeology and the Restoration of Historical Sites

Mohammed A. Alkhozai

A Historical Overview

The archipelago known as Bahrain, or Bahrain Islands, located some twenty or so miles to the east of Saudi Arabia in the middle of the Arabian Gulf, has a deep-rooted history that relates it to the ancient civilisations of the area in the second and third millennia before Christ. The region extending from present southern Iraq to the north of Oman was historically known as Bahrain. Present-day Bahrain was known as the Island of Awal at the dawn of Islam. It is worth noting that the eastern region of the Arabian Peninsula was the cradle of the ancient civilisation of Delmon. This civilisation was contemporaneous with at least four civilisations or empires of ancient times in western Asia – namely the Sumerian in Mesopotamia in the north, the Persian Empire in the east, Majan, present-day Oman to the south and that of the Indus Valley further to the east.

Owing to its central strategic location in the Gulf, the Delmon civilisation played an important connecting role between these imperial civilisations. That role may be defined as a trade intermediary or partner. Traders of Delmon were, perhaps, among the earliest seafarers in the region. They sailed the not-always-placid waters of the Gulf, transporting copper and wood from the east and returning with cargoes of dates, barley, rice and other crops.

The Delmon civilisation flourished during the zenith of the neighbouring civilisations in the region. Its proximity to Mesopotamia led it to be under the domination of this powerful empire to the north for centuries. Delmon, which was synonymous with Bahrain, appears in cuneiform records and mythological literature of Babylon. Delmon, or Tilmun as it is written in the Sumerian language, referred to the 'place from where oil was brought'.

Unlike the great civilisations of the time, the Delmon civilisation left few archaeological remains. Early settlements discovered by the Danish expedition in the 1950s at Qalat Albahrain (Bahrain Fort), and the British expedition with their excavations at Saar Settlement have revealed some remains of that civilisation.

Delmon as an auxiliary civilisation lost its importance as neighbouring empires declined. Its fame and importance diminished in the first millennium BC. It was not heard of until the rise of monotheistic faiths, as it was reduced to being just a region of the Arabian Peninsula, but, with the rise of Islamic culture, Bahrain was reinstated in history and geography. Its fertile land with abundant fresh water, vegetation and, above all, its valued marine wealth of fish and pearls, made Bahrain a target not only for its neighbours, but also the emerging empires of the West. Invaders came and went until late in the eighteenth century when the Al Khalifa, an Arabian tribe originating in Najd as a clan of 'Aniza, invaded the island and ousted its Persian governor. It established a dynasty and entered into a treaty of protection with the British. With Al Khalifa rule, political stability was maintained and peace ensured by the presence of the British Royal Navy. The island prospered once again on transit trade until the discovery of oil in the early 1930s. The winds of modernisation began to blow and the society came to be known for its tolerance and openness.

Bahrain remained as a protectorate until 1970, when the British granted the country its independence along with other Arabian Gulf sheikhdoms. Culture and heritage was one of the areas that the government patronised directly as well as through art societies. The Ministry of Information as an administrator and patron of the arts played a pivotal role in fostering arts and culture, including archaeology and antiquities, the subject of this chapter. The Department of Archaeology and Antiquities regulated excavations and archaeological expeditions invited to excavate on the island, whereas the Directorate of Museums was charged with displaying archaeological finds. An aspect of cultural development in Bahrain that deserves highlighting is the preservation, restoration and maintenance of archaeological sites and historical buildings. The process started in the 1980s. The government of Bahrain approved a plan devised by the Ministry of Information to restore, repair and rebuild monuments and historical buildings, including the Portuguese Fort, Arad Fort, Riffa' Fort, Sheikh Isa's House and Aljasra House.

The Culture and Heritage Sector of the Ministry of Information, headed by Shaikha Mai bint Mohammed Al Khalifa, continues to play a major role in implementing planned restorations. As a result of progress already achieved, Bahrain has been placed on the map of World Heritage. With the help of UNESCO and French archaeologists who were involved in excavation at the Portuguese fort, the UN Organisation recognised the fort as a Heritage Site of international importance. The remainder of this chapter is devoted to various descriptions of the restoration projects.

Forts and Houses

Qala't al-Bahrain

This is a military bastion built by the Portuguese in 1521 after their occupation of the island with the help of the Persian Governor of Hormuz. It is believed to have been constructed on the ruins of an original Islamic fort, which gives it its name. The fort was a symbol of one of the foreign occupations of the island. The architecture and design of the building, intended as the headquarters of the invading army, leave no shadow of doubt that it was European and built under Portuguese supervision. It remained in use by the occupying force until the beginning of the seventeenth century. It was built adjacent to the sea in the village of Janoosan on the northern part of the island of Bahrain. A military installation, it was surrounded by a moat and connected to the sea.

The fort was neglected over the years, so was in complete ruins when the Danish Archaeological Expedition started digging on

1. Portuguese Fort, Before

2. Portuguese Fort, Before

3. Portuguese Fort, After

4. Portuguese Fort, After

the tell outside the fort looking for remains of the Delmon era. As archaeologists, they were not concerned with restoration of the fort but with discovering what was underneath it. Restoration work on the fort itself began in the 1980s and lasted for several years. Now, fully restored, the fort and its surroundings are developed as a unified historical site on UNESCO's list of World Heritage Sites.

Arad Fort

Arad Fort was the second fort to be restored. It was built by the Omanis in the early nineteenth century. It is located in the village of Arad on Muharraq, the second-largest island. Like most forts it was built bordering the sea for easy maritime access. In shape, it is very similar to Qala't al-Bahrain but on a smaller scale. As it was more recent than the latter, it was in a better condition and was not highly affected by environmental changes. Restoration of this building took less time and effort. Owing to its location, it has become a prominent site for open-air performances. Its western façade serves perfectly as

5. Arad Fort, Before

6. Arad Fort, Before

a background for a platform raised as a stage for the performing arts. The fort is illuminated and has an imposing view overlooking the Bay of Arad. It is a major monument in Bahrain, competing only with the Old Quarter of the island in importance.

7. Arad Fort, After

8. Arad Fort, After

Riffa' Fort

This fort was constructed in the final decade of the eighteenth century. Unlike the others, it was positioned inland with no access to the sea. It has a prominent location on a plateau overlooking a valley. It is also known as Sheikh Salman bin Ahmad al Fateh Fort, after the second ruler in the al Khalifa dynasty. Despite its military usages, it served as headquarters for the new ruler. It may have also been utilised as residential palace. It lacks the structure of a traditional fort, particularly the four corner towers. In fact, it was more of a small citadel than a military stronghold. It has recently been restored and illuminated.

9. Riffa' Fort, Before

10. Riffa' Fort, Before

11. Riffa' Fort, After

12. Riffa' Fort, After

Sheikh Ibrahim bin Mohammed House

This is one of the oldest houses in one of the neighbourhoods in old Muharraq. It belonged to Sheikh Ibrahim bin Mohammed al Khalifa, one of Bahrain's intellectuals and men of letters. He was a well-known poet in the early decades of the twentieth century. The house itself, though not large, served as a literary salon where writers and poets of the time met. The poet's granddaughter, Sheikha Mai bint Mohammed al Khalifa, restored it and converted it into a cultural centre. Its location in old Muharraq made it very popular with visitors who admire the traditional architecture of the city, though in fact the house was not really restored to its previous form but rather rebuilt. It was turned into a small centre with a main lecture hall and library and research offices.

Rebuilding this house was the first project in a grand scheme to restore old dwellings of historical value and convert them into museums and centres. This move was highly commended and admired by the public. This centre helped to make Bahrain a tourist attraction. Sheikh Ibrahim House is located in what used to be the old capital city of Bahrain. Not far away from it, Sheikh Isa's House stands, along with its mosque, as the first home to be restored by the Ministry of Information. Unlike Sheikh Isa's, Sheikh Ibrahim House was a personal project carried out by a private citizen at the time. Due to its enormous popularity, other homes were restored through fundraising and support from corporations and business establishments.

Abdulla al-Zayed House

Within a few yards of the Sheikh Ibrahim Centre, separated by a narrow passage, stands Bayt Abdulla Azzayed (Abdulla al-Zayed House) in a row of houses overlooking an open square. The property belonged to Abdulla al-Zayed, considered the pioneer of journalism in Bahrain. He founded the first newspaper in Bahrain during the Second World War. He also introduced the first printing press and built the first open cinema. The property itself is a medium-sized two-storey town house. It has the features of traditional houses of the time with its central courtyard. The house was meticulously restored preserving its main features, albeit introducing modern amenities like electricity, air conditioning and glass roofing for the yard.

Al-Zayed House became the House of the Bahraini Press. In addition to telling the story of the local press, it also functions as a cultural centre for mounting exhibitions and organising lectures. All these houses are located within a radius of about half a mile, forming a traditional neighbourhood in a Bahraini town. The neighbourhood became a cultural and tourist attraction. Artistic creativity was utilised by cleaning up the whole area, brick-paving the alleys and painting the exterior walls of the houses. The heritage quarter undoubtedly arouses nostalgic memories in those who knew the area in their childhood.

Ibrahim al-Urrayedh House

Located in the Alhoora quarter of the capital city, Manama, this is where Bahrain's late poet Ibrahim al-Urrayedh lived in the 1940s. It was first acquired by the government and subsequently bequeathed to the nation. It was extensively renovated and exquisitely refurbished to be a museum housing the memorabilia of this prominent Bahraini poet.

The property is officially known as Ibrahim al-Urrayedh House,

13. Al-Urrayedh House of Poetry

14. Al-Urrayedh House of Poetry

Poetry House. It is more than a museum, as it is also a cultural centre in its own right. Conferences, lectures and poetry recitals are all hosted here. The centre is the pride of Alhoora quarter, one of the capital's oldest neighbourhoods.

In sum, restoration and renovation of forts and houses are just one aspect of cultural heritage preservation in Bahrain. Indeed, restoration of palaces and stately houses in various parts of Bahrain is proceeding apace, as a result of both governmental and private effort.

FIVE

The Social and Political Elements that Drive the Poetic Journey

Nimah Ismail Nawwab

'Poetry is the mirror of the ages.'

This reflective statement was drilled into our young minds as students, and I still remember its impact. It deepened a love for poetry that had begun at the age of eight as I listened to my father, a student and later lecturer at Edinburgh University, read Shakespeare to me at bedtime. This first lesson in my formal academic introduction to poetry, the 'mirror of the ages', has been reinforced with time and the realisation that poetry is the language of life.

The evolution of life, and of arts in general, including poetry, can be further appreciated when comparing the past to the present. When one reviews the rich history of the Arabian Peninsula, the profound, eloquent and evolutionary voices of our past transcend time and place through the poetic heritage of the land. In pre-Islamic Arabia, poetry reigned supreme. Poetry competitions at renowned sites such as Suq Ukaz drew poets from all parts of the area as they engaged in poetic bouts that often included work that was composed on the spot. Such work attests to the strength of the poets who passionately took part in contests that, in some cases, turned into famed prolonged rivalries. A legend of winning poems evolved, known as *al-mu'allaqat*, the hanging poems, which were rendered in gold and hung on the Ka'bah, the present-day site that over a billion Muslims face five times a day while performing their prayers. In present-day Arabia the reverence for poetry remains undiminished as poets are held in high regard. Ceremonies – social and official – such as weddings or inaugurations commence with poetry.

At this time in history, living in the Gulf countries is a unique experience – an intriguing time for those writers, journalists, photographers and artists depicting the pulse of the nation. We have experienced an accelerated, unprecedented rate of change, one that equals what other countries have gone through over a period of centuries. We have undergone what I like to term a 'quantum leap' or a time warp. Imagine a country that has been pulled from the fifteenth century straight into the twenty-first in just three decades. In all it has led to many adjustments which are reflected in our literary work. As a writer, poet and photographer growing up in Saudi Arabia, life has been a journey of discovery. One of the highlights of my work is combining the arts through poetry, writing and by rendering images in words and on paper. My journey into poetry, in particular, is an example of how much the society – be it the local Saudi or the ever-wider and closer global community – is reflected in the themes, evolutions, styles and voice of the poems.

Today, I will briefly touch on a few of the social elements and factors that shape our lives and are reflected in my work. When I first began writing, as many of us do, it was writing 'from the inside', from what one knows, and so I began with family poems but quickly moved on to poems on freedom and politics. We, in the kingdom, are essentially very private people. We often talk of issues and matters, but the closest to us are the ones we are reticent about. Some like to call this characteristic 'discretion'. For a long time we have been silent about our innermost thoughts and needs. It is a silence rooted in respect for long-standing cultural traditions. However, the same does not hold true of our younger generation. It is a generation that is more demanding, persistent and vocal, especially with the proliferation of technology.

My book, *The Unfurling*, marks what several reviewers have described as a passage into Arabian thought. The book sets off with a poem on freedom. This piece addresses freedom with an Arab flavour, and there are other pieces on global freedom, such as 'Shackled Slumberers', also included in the book.

The opening poem is entitled 'The Longing':

Freedom.
How her spirit,
Haunts,
Hooks,
Entices us all!

Freedom,
Will the time come
For my ideas to roam
Across this vast land's deserts,
Through the caverns of the Empty Quarter?

For my voice to be sent forth,
Crying out in the stillness of a quiet people,
A voice among the voiceless?

For my thoughts, that hurl around
In a never-ending spiral,
To settle
Mature, grow and flourish
In the barren wasteland of shackled minds?
Will my spirit be set free –
To soar above the undulating palm fronds?
Will my essence and heart be unfettered,

Forever
Freed,
Of man-made Thou Shall Nots?

Later on I began composing political pieces, as one cannot help being affected by the turmoil in the Middle East. My first such poem is entitled 'Awakenings'. The poem was written during the Palestinian *Intifada* in the wake of Muhammad Durrah's murder. It was picked up online and in print following its first publication and led to a flood of e-mails from all over the globe.

The war-ravaged region is teeming with tragedies that cannot but be addressed in our literature. Poems on Palestine, Iraq and Afghanistan soon followed. An example is this short piece entitled 'From Womb to Tomb'.

From Womb to Tomb
From womb to tomb,
An entire nation
Is condemned.

From womb to tomb,
The oppressed cry for an end.

An end to massacres, beatings and tyranny,
An end to repression and humiliation,
An end to the murder of young and old,
The shooting to kill or maim,
The burning of olive groves,
The destruction of homes,
The enslavement of a nation.

All cry out:
'When will it end?'
From womb to tomb it continues on, and on, and on....

Political poems were later followed by <u>poems on women.</u> These covered issues such as the choices women make, education, growing old, the veil, divorce and marriage.

The following piece starts with a quote from a piece by well-known African-American poet <u>Maya Angelou</u>, and is entitled 'Revolutions'.

'You may trod me in the very dirt
But still, like dust, I'll rise'
'Still I Rise', Maya Angelou

Revolutions

You may think of me
As silent, satisfied, quiescent
You may pull the curtains of secrecy
Enshroud me and my sisters in protective cocoons
You may smile and shove me down
In the quick sands of the dead desert
Bowed and broken
But   I   shall   rise.

The Red Sea, Persian Gulf shores
eddy and shift,
carrying the footsteps of our ancestors,
on dashing white caps,
Forgotten lives, forgotten needs
holding the softly spoken secrets
in the swirling depths of sheltering sea shells,
but   they   do   rise.

You may drown out my keening
drown out the grief of the little-known
You think that I lack dignity
lack understanding

lack a mind?
Does my questioning
does my right to mandated rights vex you ?
I   shall   rise.
Does my learning trouble you?
my initiatives, zest, life, get to you?
Out of stark stretching oases
my sisters' quiet concave calls stir
On   our   own   terms

No books, no stories, no shows
can colour the truth,
wax out
our growing tenacious, silken joint bonds

We shall dance and sing
our orchestra of life,
March in the rhythm of our shared songs
breathe out the dust,
breathe in the tangy thrilling bequests
   of our quest,
We shall rise
   we shall rise
     we shall rise

I   shall,
     we   shall
        Rise.....

Other poems cover life in the past. One such piece is 'Arabian Nights'.

When the call of the hudhud,
Echoes through the palm fronds
Carrying in their mists,

Visions, memories:
Caravans of high spirited steeds,
Crisscrossing the endless seas of sand,
Rushing through the oasis,
Free, yet under control.
....

Visions, memories:
Cascading starlight,
Casting its mild light over campsites,
The moonlight's silver shadow
Illuminating bearded faces,
Young boys thumping their feet
To the wild desert drum beat,
'Dana, ya dan dan'
Singing of the pearls in the far away gulf.
'Dana, ya dan dan.'

The warm cardamom-scented breeze
Carrying the fresh coffee aroma,
Warming, sizzling in the golden hooked pots
To the young giggling girls
Shyly peeking from behind the partitioned tent wall.

Flames flickering in the pit
Wood slowly consumed, sparks flying,
Dancing to the strain: 'dana, ya dan dan.'

The cry of the hudhud
Sweeps through the quiet morning air,
To the dawn of a new century.
Visions, memories,
Blown away by the winds of change.

* Hudhud is a bird known as the hoopoe.
** Dana refers to a type of Gulf pearl, and the refrain
'dana ya dan dan' is a popular one used in Gulf songs.

The Unfurling ends with haiku and short poems. One such piece is
entitled 'Revelation'.

> Isolated, harsh desert
>   Cracking, moaning fissures
>
> Opening onto the world
>   Can exposure be that painful?

More recent poems capture life in present-day Arabia, including
what I call business poems, some of which are sarcastic pieces on the
corporate world. It is a joy to experiment with styles, so I have added
some odes, such as 'Ode to a GPS' and 'Ode to my Camera'.

In the last few years we have all been touched by acts of terrorism, and in a country where we can still walk the streets late at night
without fear of muggings and even get our bags or wallets back intact
when lost, it is still very hard to comprehend the scale of terrorism
that has entered our lives.

Every time I return home from my travels, my heart wrenches
on seeing tanks, soldiers with guns and sandbags. It hits us on a very
emotional level to see a peaceful country being invaded in such a hor-
rific way. This led to what I call a 'phase' of writing about terrorism.
One piece on this theme is entitled 'The Ambush'. This is an excerpt
from the poem.

> As the very essence of our faith now stands in danger
> Of this ambush from within,
> Turning back upon them,
> Derailing their intentions
> As hate colours their vision of the truth,

That we are all,   all,   all
Sons and daughters of Adam

That the three faiths,
Our mainstay, our guide
Are interlinked, bonded forever
Sealed by The One
To spread   their   message   of   peace   for   human kind.

A favourite is entitled 'The Bleakest Night', which I wrote after the first terrorism attack hit our capital city. This piece has allusions to *Macbeth*.

The Bleakest Night

I

The blackest, bleakest night descended
On the land of praying palm trees.

The guardian kingdom,
Lies open and bare.

With its shattered peace, shattered innocence
In the wake of rancorous explosions.
Fair is foul, and foul is fair,
The world lies on its hinges,
Askew.

Right is wrong, and wrong is right,
The wicked work of blinded messengers of death,
Rocked the nation,
Roiled nations.

Dark deed done in the darkness of night
Under the hate-laden hovering cloud
Of fanaticism, utter ruthlessness,
Of hatred for the Other.

Future generations
Will bear the stigma,
Of weapons used to vanquish the unarmed.
Of innocent people from all creeds,
Lives torn asunder,
A blemish shared by all.
No oceans will cleanse the stain
Remembered with loathing by all.

II

The blackest, bleakest night,
Soaked with the blood of the innocents.

As demented, lethal minds,
Planned and went about their unholy work.

Cloaking their viperish, venomous deed,
In the name of a peaceful religion.

Carrying out the mission of death,
Death of Muslim-mandated tolerance,
Death of historic ties with the People of the Book.
Death of illustrious Islamic honour,
Death of long-held values,
Death of the essence of their faith.

Attempting to shake the very name,

The venerated spirit of 'Salam', of peace.
The peaceful in 'Islam'
Ripped out of the word,
Ripped out of their merciful faith.

A molten lava of bitterness,
Spewing forth resentment,
Sowing the seeds of anarchy.

Fanaticism rearing its ugly head,
Brazenly flouting the very principles Islam espouses,
Of equality in the eyes of the One.
Dealing the death blow to their pious calling,
Exposing their warped thinking to the world.

Their people, their land refute them,
Consigning them and their arcane act to the devil.

Will the bleakest night ever be forgotten?

I would like to end on a lighter note, so here is a passage from a piece about global education called 'Recipe for Knowledge'.

Open up canned books
Fork out the subjects
Spread out the math, science, history, literature,
Slather with flowery phrases,
Mix in tongue-twisting passages,
Spice up with lengthy, peppery pages,
Heat, simmer till dried into a solid mass
Of intimidating, mysterious tomes
Cool, and turn on their sides,
Brush with the yolk of white wishy-washy learning.

Measure in years of memorising,
Pick over each word carefully,
Dice up creativity into slim, slim slivers,
Sift and wipe clean of creativity,
Prune and slash threatening questions,
Beat in harshness, discipline,
Mix it well; mix it well.

Add mandated narrow dogmas,
Sift out other approaches,
Skewer systematic planning,
Wash away the roots of ingenuity,
Scoop out criticism,
Stuff the tender shoots, receptive brains
With reams of evaporated needless figures and facts,
Freeze   for   decades.

In the light of the way poetry is evolving and continues to draw audiences through its emotional impact, even in these days of speed and constant distractions, it is imperative to realise that the passion that drives poets can serve us all. Can poetry put an end to child slavery, human trafficking, abuse, poverty? Can it eradicate diseases such as HIV, or end wars? No. Does poetry portray the sorrow of other human beings and the source of their suffering? Yes. Does it cross borders in these traumatic times? Absolutely.

Poetry bridges gaps and helps us celebrate and embrace differences. Poetry strengthens the facets that make us all human.

SIX

Sport and Identity in the Gulf

Abdullah Baabood

Introduction

Sport and culture have become increasingly prominent in contemporary society and one of the most relevant features of sport is that it is an essential part of popular culture. It is widely recognised that sports and leisure occupy an ever more central and visible place at the heart of a global consumer and media culture. With the recent expansion of the cultural industries, sport's national and global profile and its contribution to the expression of personal, cultural and national identity are ever greater.[1]

At the national level, where a shared language, educational system and mass media of information have become vital cultural tools for disseminating senses of modern nationhood, sport is regularly used as an expression of national sentiment.[2] Sport is commonly viewed as a mechanism of national solidarity promoting a sense of identity, unity, stature and esteem. At a range of major sporting events, fans arrive waving and draping themselves in their national flags and with their faces painted in national colours.

Globally, sport has become a cultural bond that links countries across national boundaries. It provides a common enthusiasm and shared empathic experiences that transcend national allegiances and generally provides opportunities for relationship, friendship, understanding and goodwill. But, on the other hand, sport is also a means of identity differentiation and even confrontation between nations, at times instigating aggression, stereotyping and images of inferiority and superiority.

Although it was thought that globalisation impulses would diminish the significance of national identity in general, thus simultaneously weakening the links between sports and the expression of nationalism, the relationship between sport, national identity and nationalism today remains as strong as ever.[3] Politicians are willing to use and harness sports for their own ends. For example, in the United Kingdom John Major chose the game of cricket as quintessentially English, and Norman Tebbit claimed that a test on allegiance to national cricket teams should apply to ethnic minorities in Britain. In France, Jean-Marie Le Pen, leader of the National Front, complained that it was inauthentic to choose football players from abroad and seek to present them as an authentically French team at the World Cup finals in 1988.[4]

It has been said that identity is 'an individual's or a group's sense of self' and it refers to the images of individuality and distinctiveness ('selfhood') held and projected by an actor and formed (and modified over time) through relationships with significant 'others'.[5] Identity, though, is not a single homogenous stock of traits, images and habits.[6] Individuals, and to a lesser extent groups, carry multiple identities that are by definition variable. It has become virtually self-evident that identity is overwhelmingly constructed and that identities are formed in a number of different locations and social practices. Specifically, sport is clearly linked to the construction and reproduction of specific sub-national identities among many people – as, for example, masculinity, or social class.[7] Moreover, the celebratory dimension of sports reveals the fundamental link between popular culture and identity with implications that transgress by far the limits of sport as a mere private leisure activity. The intensification of commercialisation and the growth of mass communication have fundamentally changed the face of sport from being an amateur vocation, a leisure pursuit and a source of recreation to a professional occupation as well as a source of celebrity and business status.

Sports Culture and Gulf Identity

For Saudi Arabia, the GCC states and the whole of the Middle East, there is generally a fundamental problem with national identity. These states have not completely succeeded in evolving a national identity that cohesively reflects their heterogeneity.[8] None of the Middle East states is homogenous; they consist of numerous ethnic, religious, cultural and linguistic minorities.[9] Most, if not all, of the Middle East states have not been able to address, let alone resolve, the core issue of national identity which in some cases has resulted in schism and sectarian tensions. They are, in fact, states still in search of nation-hood and they tend to undertake numerous means of circumventing the problem of national identity. They have a propensity to impose identity from above using ideological, religious, dynastic or power political diktats. National identity in the Gulf is thus a political issue as these states are preoccupied with preserving some cultural autonomy and the maintenance of a trans-national, as well as a purely Arabic and Islamic, national character.[10] Sport is one of the most powerful means of generating this identity which explains officialdom's interest in and support of the phenomenon.

The growing global nature of sport and the cultural identity appeal that is enhanced by the business sponsorships and advertisements attached to it have found a receptive fertile ground in the Gulf region. Indeed, the sports culture of the Gulf states today combines both the traditional sports of nomadic Arabian society with contemporary sports of Western origin. There are traditional sports of enduring popularity including dhow, camel and horse racing which are very popular and held throughout the region. An enormous amount of money has recently been invested in the latter sport; indeed, Arabian horses are held to be among the finest in the world. Falconry is enjoyed primarily by wealthy sheikhs: although hunting with guns is now generally banned, traditional hunting (with hounds or falcons) is still popular. Some old traditional and folklore sports encouraged by governments are returning to popularity as one means of reinforcing cultural identity.

The Gulf states, not traditionally known for their modern sporting culture, have over the last few decades been encouraging sports generously, helped by oil revenues. More recently, modern sports have been rapidly finding their way to the Gulf because of the wealth being created there and because of governments' deliberate policies. As many modern nations out of necessity seek fresh ways of unifying disparate people into some manner of 'imaginary community',[11] the Gulf states, with their recent development, are reinventing themselves and redefining their national identity. As sport is one important medium, the Gulf countries have been trying to organise and even localise many of the modern sports. Moreover, sport in the Gulf has become a major component of the Gulf economic diversification plan and is becoming a tool for leaders in the region to redefine their identities and to reposition their countries on the world map.

All GCC states already boast a number of sports facilities such as large stadiums capable of hosting international competitions. GCC governments promote sports through physical education in public schools and the establishment of huge sports complexes in large urban centres, smaller neighbourhood sports centres, and sports clubs in rural areas. Moreover, GCC states also host a number of world-class sporting events; more are being planned for the future with massive investments in infrastructure and the management of these events. For example, Qatar has now become the regional venue for the World Superbike Championship, motor cycling's equivalent of Formula One, and the country has also hosted a $1.5 million Qatar Exxon Mobil Open for men in January 2007 and the Qatar TotalFinaElf Open for women in February and March 2007 approved by the Association of Tennis Players and the Women's Tennis Association.[12]

Doha in 2004 created the Academy for Sports Excellence ASPIRE, the largest indoor facility of its kind in the world. Covering an astounding 290,000 square metres of ground space and standing at an impressive 46 metres high, it seats 15,000 spectators.[13] Designed by Roger Taillibert – the architect behind the Parc des Princes Stadium in Paris and the Olympic Stadium in Montreal, Canada – the Dome was constructed over two years. The state-of-the-art steel structure houses an Olympic-sized swimming pool and diving area, a 200-metre athletics track, a gymnastics hall, a games hall, a full-sized football field and a five-a-side pitch, eleven tennis courts, thirteen table tennis courts, eight fencing strips, two squash courts and a wood-floored judo and karate studio. Under the Dome's distinctive sloping roof and the architecturally mesmerising Academy, there are also lecture halls, classrooms, science laboratories, dormitories, a library, an amphitheatre and a medical centre. The ASPIRE opening ceremony was marked by the Middle East's biggest-ever celebration of sporting achievement, attended by legendary sports stars such as Pelé and Diego Maradona, Olympic delegations from over eighty countries, and representatives from other major sports federations such as the International Association of Athletics Federations.

Qatar also played host to the 15th Asian Games from 1 to 15 December 2006. This GCC country was the first Arab Middle Eastern country to host this major international multi-sport event representing forty-five countries (comprising about two-thirds of the world's population) and thirty-nine sports (eleven more than the Olympics), involving more than 12,500 athletes – 1,500 more than the Olympics.[14] For this Doha invested more than $2.8 billion in developing the necessary infrastructure, including $800 million on the Khalifa Sports City, which features the $300 million Khalifa Stadium, and $700 million on an athletes' village, beating heavyweights Hong Kong, Kuala Lumpur and New Delhi.[15]

The Asian Games were expected to benefit the future economic development of the country, especially the construction, hospitality, travel and tourism sectors. For example, the Asian Games is thought to have added about 1,000 additional hotel rooms to the 2,600 previously available. This is in addition to the 20 percent expansion in Qatar's residential stock. During the first two weeks of December, Qatar was featured in newspapers and on television screens around the world to over a billion people.[16] Like the Olympics, the Games are also an effort to promote a pan-Asian identity transcending political, cultural and religious differences. A photographic exhibition along Doha's waterfront was entitled the 'Unity of Asia', calling Asia 'our common home'.[17]

'While sports have become a key part of Qatar's identity, the nation's athletics door did not close when the torch left Doha on 15 December for Ghangzhou, China where the next Games take place in 2010.'[18] In September 2006, Doha announced an interest in bidding for the right to host the 2016 Olympic Games, bringing it into direct competition with Dubai and eleven other cities around the world which had also expressed interest in hosting the world's biggest sporting spectacle.[19] The director general of the Doha Asian Games Organising Committee (DAGOC) revealed that Qatar was developing plans to host the Olympic Games. He said that 'we are preparing the bid report for the 2016 Olympics and are confident of hosting such a big event if given the opportunity', and added, 'Our aim is to be a centre of excellence for sport in the Middle East and later in Asia.'[20]

In the same vein, the Qatar National Olympic Committee's general secretary announced that Doha is to bid to host the Football World Cup in 2018, and could invite neighbouring countries to join in as co-hosts.[21] The news that this small Gulf state is preparing to bid for the world's biggest sporting events highlights the growing importance of sport to the Gulf; the Doha Asian Games are just the beginning.

Bahrain also has invested around $300 million to build the Formula One Grand Prix Bahrain Racing Circuit (BRC) at Sakhir, a landmark example for the region. The event has more than 200 million viewers worldwide and its returns are estimated at about $75 million.[22] The Bahraini government has been counting specifically on creating a sports culture and a motor heritage that would fill up the rest of the calendar year. The track has not just brought Formula One, but has developed an automotive side business.[23] Bahrain has also staged the World Volleyball Championship.

But nowhere has this aggressive rebranding of the region been more evident than in Dubai. As a regional leader in the field of using sports as a powerful mechanism, Dubai has opted for a serious redefinition and rebranding of its image, using some of the world's leading sportspersons to promote its sporting credentials. For example, world number one tennis player Roger Federer played Andre Agassi in a high-profile publicity stunt in 2005, on the rooftop helipad of the iconic Burj al-Arab hotel. The world's top golfer, Tiger Woods, has also been used to promote events in Dubai.[24]

In order to promote its identity, the Dubai government also works hand in hand with its national air carrier Emirates, not only to bring spectators and reduce costs for organisers, but to market the city's potential and image internationally. Its $150 million sponsorship deal with London's Arsenal Football Club in 2005 has been just one of dozens of seven-year sponsorship deals around the world that it has concluded over the last two years, covering cricket, Formula One and even Australian Rules Football. The airline has also signed a $195 million sponsorship deal with World Football's governing body FIFA from 2007 to 2014, for a period that includes World Cup finals.

Dubai, moreover, is planning an Autodrome and Business Park – which is expected to bring the top names in the global racing circuits to the emirate. Dubai has also tapped a new scheme under the A1 Grand Prix model, in which teams representing each participating country will buy franchises for between $5 million and $150 million to race one of the thirty 3.5-litre cars designed by Lola Cars International of the UK.

Among the other high-profile events that the region has been hosting are the Dubai Desert Classic – a part of the premier Professional

Golf Association tour – with prize money of $2 million and attracting the world's best players and the media fraternity; the $1.6 million Dubai Tennis Championship; International Rugby Board Sevens; the Dubai World Cup, offering total prize money of $15.25 million and featuring the world's richest horse race. Dubai's Godolphin stable now dominates international horse racing around the world. The 1999 Bowling World Cup Championship and the 2003 FIFA Youth World Cup were also held in the UAE.

Given its enthusiasm for sports and its promotional spin-offs, Dubai is building for $3 billion the world's first integrated sports city. This will cover approximately 50 million square feet and feature state-of-the-art stadiums and world-class sporting academies, schools, shops, restaurants, hotels, a hospital and other essential services and facilities. It consists of a 60,000-seat outdoor stadium, a 25,000-seat cricket stadium, a 10,000-seat indoor arena, a 5,000- to 10,000-seat field hockey and athletics venue, a signature eighteen-hole golf course designed by Ernie Els, a Butch Harmon golf academy, the first Manchester United soccer school outside Europe, and a David Lloyd tennis school, among other things.[25] It also includes access to state-of-the-art stadia and other world-class sports and entertainment venues. Additional facilities include international schools, medical facilities, emergency services, parks, playgrounds, hotels and hundreds of retail opportunities.[26]

Other events that have become a regular feature on the UAE sporting calendar are the Abu Dhabi Golf Championship, which is part of the European PGA Tour and the World Endurance Race and the Formula One Power Boat Championship. Abu Dhabi has also built a multi-million-dollar cricket stadium that has hosted several international fixtures.

Sharjah announced in December 2006 the building of a sports city worth Dh650 million in addition to a sport education college that will be part of the University of Sharjah. It has also established itself in the region in cricket with the Sharjah's Cricketers Benefit Fund Scheme series. Cricket 'for the people of Sharjah, it had a dimension beyond that of pure entertainment, for it gave them a sense of identity. Here they could watch their heroes in the flesh and identify with them at first hand.'[27] While cricket is hardly played by the indigenous population there are, however, due to the internationalisation of the Gulf, millions involved in the various tournaments organised for cricket fans, who are mostly expatriate residents and who have become part of the Gulf landscape. Moreover, the International Cricket Council has shifted its headquarters from London to Dubai for tax purposes. In fact, cricket business in the region has expanded to give birth to Ten Sports – a product of Taj Television Ltd, the Dubai Media City-based company targeting millions of homes, mostly in the region and on the Indian subcontinent.[28]

Even Saudi Arabia has climbed onto the bandwagon by introducing the Hail Rally, and Oman is also organising the Oman Rally which is part of the Middle East Rally Championship and is hoping to host a round of the World Rally Championship (WRC). According to the Olympic Council of Asia, Oman is also hosting the Asian Beach Games in 2010.[29]

The cost of holding such events is enormous and is frequently held up as an argument against bidding to host them. However, hosting these big events is really not about return on investment. They are never going to make a profit, whatever they do. One cannot imagine how these states will recoup even a fraction of their costs despite broadcast rights, sponsorship and ticketing. The main motivator for this large investment and increasing interest in sport is that they provide a means whereby these states can engage with the rest of the world, to showcase their modern culture, express their national identity and project their self-image by reiterating in a big way what Mohammad al-Rumiahi had said about twenty years ago, that, 'The Gulf is not just oil'.[30] It is also about engagement with the rest of the world and, in the words of the Qatar Sports Press Committee president, 'We are looking to be part of the world and create friendship with others. There has been no civilisation without sport.'[31]

Indeed, the effect of globalisation, with its high increase in the flow of goods and images and the presence of a disproportionate number of foreign workers in the Gulf, where citizens have, in some cases, become minorities in their own homeland, presents a serious threat to the societal culture and national identity.[32] The increasing population is tilted more towards the younger generation and, in the absence of democratic representative governments, presents another challenge to the GCC governments.[33] Sport not only keeps the young generation preoccupied but it also provides a large dose of immunisation against foreign culture and a protection against loss of national identity.

Obviously, showcasing the state and its image and identity has a long-term economic benefit and promotional dividend. Sport is also seen as another way of attracting more people to visit the region for tourism, trade and investment. Ireland's hosting of the Ryder Cup is a good example. The event itself made a profit, but it also brought thousands of people who put their money into the economy and created an identity for the country.[34]

The chief beneficiaries of all these sporting activities are sports people and their fans together with the tourism, construction and services sectors. Airlines, hotels, all types of leasing apartments, advertising firms and car rental agencies experience the spill-over effect. The infrastructural projects that result from these developments keep the economy ticking and vibrant. They also have a robust impact on the GDP growth rates in the region, apart from generating job opportunities, especially as unemployment has become a serious concern to the regional governments.

Building or investing in new sports infrastructure, and hosting these global sporting events with the presence of international sportspersons and sports celebrities, not only put the regional countries on the world tourism map, but also serve to promote a safe and good image of a stable environment – a crucial criterion for tourists and investors alike. Fukuyama, for example, contends that Germany's hosting of the World Cup has precipitated a much more robust public debate about national identity. He asserts that 'during last year's successful soccer World Cup, the widespread expression of moderate national feeling became completely normal, and was even welcomed by Germany's neighbours'.[35]

On the other side of the coin, the spin-off of such development and investment in sports on the Gulf population and particularly its possible negative effect on local culture is yet to be revealed. There is no doubt that there is going to be an impact on the local culture which has given some conservatives reason to voice their concerns over the adverse effects of hosting these events.[36]

Gulf Identity and Sporting Elites

The elites and ruling families have been at the forefront of driving the culture of sports in the region. Their large investments and their patronage of many of the sporting ventures, local sports people and sporting events, has been aimed at building a sporting culture and producing a local identity.

At an almost unprecedented level, some of the Arab elites have themselves been showing the way to aspiring younger generations. Some of the ruling families' younger members have been revealing quite a bit of sportsmanship and talent. This has been mostly noted in Dubai's Al Maktoum family, the horse-loving Al Nahayans and Qatar's young Al Thanis, who have had several of their young members win sporting medals. Sheikh Rashid, the eldest son (aged twenty-five) of Sheikh Mohammed, the Ruler of Dubai, has won gold medals in the 120-kilometre individual endurance ride and the 120-kilometre team ride. He led his brothers – Sheikh Hamdan, Ahmed and Majid – in the team event, creating sporting history as the first quartet of brothers to appear together.

All four are experienced equestrians: Sheikh Ahmed won the 2002 Endurance World Championship in Spain, at the age of fifteen. Rashid's victory in the individual race was his twenty-seventh win since 1977. Their sister, Sheikha Miatha, took a silver medal in martial arts (kumite) at the Doha games and she intends to support the sport among women in the UAE. Another female cousin from a different branch of the family has won prizes, Sheikha Latifa having taken a bronze medal in the showjumping event. Their cousin, Saeed Al Maktoum, the eldest son of Sheikh Maktoum Bin Rashid, the former ruler of Dubai, is well known for his promotion of sports. He chairs the Al-Shabab sports club in Dubai and took the silver medal in shooting at the Asian Games in Doha. Sheikh Maktoum Hasher Al Maktoum, known for his passion and investments in automotive sports, founded the A1 Grand Prix.

The Al Nahayan siblings – Sheikhs Hazza and Khalid and Sheikhas Alyazia and Shamma, sons and daughters of the UAE Prime Minister Sheikh Sultan Bin Zayed Al Nahayan – are also regular competitors in endurance racing. Hazza won the 2005 FEI Endurance World Championship.

Two of Bahrain's King Hamad Bin Isa Al Khalifa's sons also won medals in Doha. A fourth son, Bahrain Royal Equestrian and Endurance Federation (BREEF) president Sheikh Nasser, took the endurance individual silver medal and he and his younger brother were members of the team that also took the endurance silver.

In Qatar, three of Emir Sheikh Hamad's sons (including the heir apparent) played a key role in preparing for the Asian Games. One of them was named Asian Games Torch Relay Ambassador. A fourth son, Sheikh Mohammed, took centre stage at the Asian Games opening ceremony. As a talented equestrian, he rode his horse up a ramp the height of the stadium to light the Games cauldron.[37]

Football and the Gulf

Sports events, especially football (soccer) matches, have become the most important contributors to popular culture and national identity. Football is one of the greatest cultural institutions, like education and mass media, which shape and cement national identities throughout the world. Football is the most popular spectator sport in the world, and it is a game where humanity comes alive with one goal.[38]

Football has always remained a symbol of various sorts of identities and cultural marker of different nationalities. 'Behind the façade of its obvious entertainment aspect, it has proved to be a perpetuating reflector of cultural nationalism, distinctive ethnicity, community or communal identity, cultural specificity as well as representative of models of development and international status of the post-colonial nation state.'[39]

Football is also sometimes intimately intertwined with both domestic and international politics.[40] Even for those nations that still remain outside the mainstream of world football, such as the GCC states, the game still has much appeal and offers potential for commercialisation, as well as opportunities for generating foreign investments and for flexing economic muscle.[41]

The differentiation and the classification of the game, the characterisation of the event as a 'national', 'regional' or 'international' game in public opinion and in media hype, also play a critical role in transforming the football culture of nations. Indeed, football teams from different parts of the country may represent rival localities with no small amount of fierce competition. While the competition largely remains within the unifying framework of a national league system, there can be cases of conflict and split loyalty.[42] At international levels, however, the team embodies the modern nation-state, often literally wrapping itself in the national flag – no one has waved the flag more eagerly than football fans, and matches begin lustily with the communal singing of the 'national anthem'.

The power of the new media ensures that every corner of the nation can share the action (and thus participate) by watching on television or listening to the radio.[43] The whole nation, with its different socio-economic classes and generations (the young, the old, the rich and the poor), can come together, go through the same experience and share the same feelings. The 'symbolic' shirts that the supporters wear, the colours on faces, the flag waving, the passion and devotion of football singing, chanting, and hugging amongst complete strangers illustrate this unity. Football even has its fundamentalists and 'hooligans' that go to the extreme of using violence to illustrate their devotion, by fighting in the name of their team with rival fans. Some would even claim that all of these seem to be attributes of a 'new tribalism', or even form what appear to be a new religion and, most importantly, a faith![44] Clearly, for some, football is more than simply a game of two teams, and in the words of the great Liverpool legend, Bill Shankly: 'Some people think football is a matter of life and death. I can assure them, it is much more serious than that.'[45] Football clearly has tribalism associated with religion. Whatever the comparison, football engages people in a mass, emotional display of faith and collective strength just as many religions or tribes do.

In fact, the appeal and popularity of football originate from the nature of the game itself and from its essential features – the relative simplicity of its rules, equipment and body techniques. Its historical development has also added to its popularity, as the game was transmitted through trade and educational routes rather than through a directly imperial relationship and it therefore lacked any hegemonic strings. Its early development might be regarded as one of the earliest forms of cultural globalisation because, unlike cricket or rugby union, the introduction of football into other cultures did not necessitate any capitulation by other natives to British political or economic rules. As the game developed in some parts of the world, football soon became a vehicle for cultural pride, ethnic solidarity and the national identity of the indigenous peoples.

 In the GCC states, as has generally been the case elsewhere, football – as the game of the poor and the underprivileged – has been dominated by working-class players and largely by players from migrant backgrounds, some of them of second or third generations. Football popularity and professionalism offered these players a route towards social recognition within a meritocratic environment, and life-chance opportunities that were denied elsewhere, in politics, commerce and higher education. Sponsorships and advertising have further catapulted players from mere sports heroes to stars and celebrities.

In the Gulf, as in most countries around the world, no other sport enjoys the immense popularity of football. Football in the Gulf dates back to the arrival of British forces and traders to the region. However, it was only during the 1950s that the game began to become more organised, with the initiation of various football associations and tournaments such as the Gulf Cup. The GCC states have been spending generously on building the infrastructure for football, in supporting local football clubs and especially their national teams. Among the most successful is Saudi Arabia's national team which has won the Asian Cup three times, in 1984, 1988 and 1996. They won the World Under-17 Championship in 1989 and qualified four times for the World Cup. The Kuwaiti national team also took part in the 1982 World Cup finals and two Asian Cups, reaching the finals in 1976 and taking home the winner's trophy in 1980. Kuwait also took part at the Sydney 2000 Olympic Games.

The Gulf Cup

The Gulf Cup is a football championship tournament held every two years between the nations of the Gulf. The idea originated with an initiative from the Bahrain Football Federation while attending the summer Olympics in 1986. Saudi opinion was sought, and a subsequent meeting was held in Manama between Saudi Arabia, Kuwait and Qatar and, of course, Bahrain, where the idea was approved. The first round of the Gulf Cup was held between 27 March and 3 April 1970.

The United Arab Emirates joined in the next round in 1972, Oman in the third round in 1974, Iraq in the fourth round in 1976 and, following the admission of the Yemen to some of the GCC bodies including sports, Yemen joined the Gulf Cup competition in 2004. Besides football, other sports like basketball, handball and volleyball were added later to the seventeenth and the eighteenth stagings of the tournament, in Qatar in 2004 and the UAE in 2006.

The Gulf Cup has a special place in the Gulf region and is a distinguished tournament among regional and international sports events. Being held between neighbouring countries it has a unique flavour as it evokes a lot of passion and pride from sports fans in the region. There is a great deal of media intensity, a large amount of attention and money spent on promoting the national teams, including bringing international foreign coaches and, in some cases, even naturalising foreign players who are added to the national team. In replying to critics of foreign players, the president of the Qatar Sports Press Committee said, 'It is legal to bring athletes from outside the country. Much of the world does it. We are a small nation, and to get results we need stars.'[46] There has also been a lot of expectation, joy and tears, songs, poems, tragedies, humiliation, sacking and/or resignations of officials and coaches – and even parliamentary debates and investigations into failure and corruption. The idea that these neighbouring states' national teams meet to compete at this level has an overwhelming influence on public culture and identity. The name of the Gulf Cup has a uniting effect, on one hand, for the people of the Gulf and Yemen. However, as the competition pits one country's national team against another's, there are also strong individual national senses of identity within the overall Gulf (Khaliji) identity. Many of the supporters, including women, wrap themselves in national flags and colour their hair and faces with the national colours.

The whole country naturally supports its national team while playing but in case of an early exit fans tend to choose one of their other favourite teams to support. The intensity of the competition and the media hype keep the public engaged with the sport even if their national team is out of it. Over its thirty-six-year championship history, Kuwait has dominated, winning nine times, followed by Saudi Arabia with three victories, Iraq with three, Qatar two, and United Arab Emirates one. Oman, Bahrain and Yemen are yet to win the championship, although Oman has played in the last two finals. This last fact is remarkable, given that Oman was the last country in the Gulf to open up to the outside world and that, until the 1970s, football or any public sport was banned by the reclusive sultan. Oman managed to stay at the bottom of the league table for many years, but that position is now held by Yemen, reflecting its late entry into the tournament as well as its limited resources. The fact that the Omani national team reached the final on the last two occasions and came close to touching the Cup is something that makes Omanis proud of their national team's performance to the extent that there was a huge public celebration even though they were runners-up.

The national teams that wear the colour of their national flag have become known by (and nicknamed for) their colours. For example the Saudi Arabia national team is known as al-Akhdar which means 'The Green(s)'. Qatar is al-Anabi 'The Maroon(s)'. Oman and Bahrain are al-Ahmar, 'The Red(s)' and UAE, al-Abyadh, are 'The White(s)'.

Curiously, neither Saudi Arabia nor, more particularly, Kuwait has been performing as well recently. Disappointed with their national team performance, the Kuwaiti public has started calling their team al-Ozairaq ('The Blu-ish'), which is belittling in Arabic, considering their famous al-Azraq ('The Blues') has the best record of wins and goals in the Gulf Cup. Moreover, Kuwait's recent relatively poor performance in the Gulf Cup has sparked strong public debates, resignation of senior sports personalities and even parliamentary questions.[47]

The UAE played the host nation for the eighteenth Gulf Cup tournament in January 2007. The opening ceremony was held at a state-of-the-art stadium with fireworks, breathtaking acrobatics, flag raising, creating the portrait of Sheikh Khalifa, President of the UAE, on a huge white cloth, a parade of military men and highlighting the story of the life of the Bedouin, sitting in front of his tent with his camel in the desert. The huge gathering showed the importance and the popularity of the tournament: 60,000 spectators were at the stadium and millions watched the opening match between Oman and UAE – which Oman won 2–1 – on television.

Despite this initial setback, the UAE managed to reach the final, beating Oman 1–0, and winning the tournament for the first time in their history. The win was significant for the identity of this newly formed country and an important boost for national feelings and a support to local identity. The UAE only came into being in the early 1970s. Nowhere in the Gulf have local culture and identity been more threatened than they are in the UAE, especially in Dubai because of the large imbalance between the smaller local indigenous population and the huge expatriate population.

Thrilled by his national team's performance, Sheikh Mohammed Bin Rashid Al Maktoum, Vice President and ruler of Dubai, leapt up beaming with jubilation in the stadium when the first and only goal was struck. Sheikh Mohammed, commenting later, emphasised that all the people who were at the stadium were engaging with the game immensely. 'This interaction was natural and reflected the true national feelings, which led me to jump out of my chair when UAE scored against Oman.'[48]

There was high-level involvement of the ruling elite along with the masses in supporting the national team and cheering it along. Large prize money was promised and given to individual players for scoring goals and to the team for winning games. The UAE team ultimately presented the cup to Sheikh Khalifa bin Zayed Al Nahayan, the ruler of Abu Dhabi and President of the UAE, just as the whole team had stood in front of him and saluted him from the field when they had scored the winning goal.

Sheikh Mohammed led a procession for the players in Dubai after a previous procession in Abu Dhabi. UAE people from all the seven emirates came to Dubai to celebrate the victory of their team at the Gulf Cup and people hugged and congratulated each other in the streets. In Dubai, a huge rally started spontaneously and thousands of cars with klaxons roamed through the streets joyously spraying foam, with headlights going crazy, flags out from windows and almost everyone in a totally celebratory mood. Traffic came to a standstill in many places. The happy nation paraded through the city of Dubai after they had done the same in Abu Dhabi on the previous day, dancing in the streets to the sound of national songs pouring out of all the cars. Many fans were seen on the tops of the cars dancing jubilantly.

The procession started from Zabeel Palace, where they were joined by Sheikh Mohammed and moved onto roads throughout Dubai. The team members, all together on a truck and holding the Gulf Cup aloft, led the caravan. The final destination was to be the Global Village where the UAE Football Federation held a musical concert. Along the way, the rally split into two caravans, one taking the victory parade route, starting from Zabeel, through Sheikh Zayed Road, Jumeirah Road and onwards, while the other headed straight for the Global Village where the final celebrations started at 7.00 PM. 'The noise was incredible, with police sirens, cars honking and girls screaming,' said one resident, who said he was happy to share in the joy.[49]

At the Global Village, Gate No. 1 was kept open exclusively for the players in the bus and for those cars that had been decorated specially for the occasion. All other vehicles were allowed only through one other gate, which created an enormous traffic jam. The players were received by officials of the Dubai Shopping Festival. Many four-wheelers were decorated with graffiti and sprayed with the words, 'I love you Whites' in Arabic. The celebrations went on till 1.00 AM. Some of the top names on the Arab pop scene, such as Ahlam, Abdullah Bil Khair, Fayez Saeed, Hamad al-Ameri, Arayam and Samr sang and danced through the night with the joyous crowd.[50]

The Dubai Sports Channel began a campaign for donations to be given to the UAE national football team for being champions of the Gulf Cup. The studio and offices of the TV channel had been receiving donations through direct telephone calls, e-mails and faxes. Three- to four-day celebrations were held in the country and the emirates: the public – including women and children – were out on the streets. Some people were in traditional dress, smoking water pipes.

Dubai Sports Channel, prominent among other emirates stations for broadcasting the Gulf Cup events live, stayed on the air for at least three days after the match final, airing live shows of the celebrations and interviews with dignitaries, players and the public. The public inundated the television channel with messages and poems, which were broadcast, praising the national team and its historical achievement. Sheikh Mohammed himself wrote a poem for the occasion.

Sheikh Khalifa Bin Zayed Al Nahayan, the President of the UAE, instructed that Dh500,000 be given to each player of the UAE football team for winning the eighteenth Gulf Cup championship.[51] In addition, Sheikh Mohammed Bin Rashid Al Maktoum, Vice-President and Prime Minister of the UAE and ruler of Dubai, awarded each member of the victorious UAE team a villa in their respective emirates.[52] Sheikh Mohammed's wife undertook to send the whole team on *umrah* at her own expense. Religious tokens included a Qur'an given to each one of the team and a sura from the Qur'an from a prisoner, in response to which the team planned to visit the prison and asked the rulers for leniency with prison sentences. The public raised funds and donations and the elites and business people threw lavish parties and gave generously to the team.

Sheikh Mohammed, who welcomed the members of the victorious team, the head and members of the UAE Football Association and other officials to his Zabeel Palace, congratulated and commended the team spirit which had led the team to victory making everyone – from the leaders to all the people of the country – very happy. Sheikh Mohammed spoke to the team members with the combined warm feelings of a sportsman, human being, and leader keen for the advancement of his nation and people on all possible levels. Sheikh Mohammed said: 'You have done a good job. I asked you to be lions, you truly became the lions of the football stadium, especially in the presence of President His Highness Sheikh Khalifa Bin Zayed Al Nahayan, in my presence and that of most of the UAE sheikhs, ministers and UAE people. Everyone did a great job in encouraging you to succeed.'[53] To show the high level of his involvement in preparing the national team he added that, 'I was in constant communication with the officials of the Football Association, especially Sheikh Abdullah Bin Zayed Al Nahayan, Minister of Foreign Affairs and the head of the UAE FA General Assembly, to inquire about your training and performance.'[54] Sheikh Mohammad also reminded the team of his directives during his visit to the team's training camp at the Abu Dhabi Hilton the previous Ramadan.

Conclusion

Sports play an important role as a cultural and identity marker for many nations. The Gulf states, grappling with their identity, particularly amid the effects of globalisation and their sociopolitical and economic needs, have used sport to help establish their individual cultural and national identities. The GCC governments have encouraged traditional sports as well as spending a great deal of their wealth on promoting modern sports in the region. Ruling families in the GCC have been at the forefront, promoting sports, and some of the young ruling elites are leading by example in their sporting ambitions.

Despite the high spending on a variety of modern sports infrastructure and the hosting of many types of competitions, football remains the most popular sport in the GCC. The Gulf Cup tournament is the regional apex of football competitions and is effectively a derby between the neighbouring GCC member states as well as Iraq and Yemen. The Gulf Cup enjoys a high level of both official and public support and unleashes public feelings and national sentiments. Along with other international sporting events held in the region, it helps to promote popular Gulf culture and bolster national identity and the image of the GCC states.

Notes

1. Emma Poulton, 'Mediated Patriot Games, The Construction and Representation of National Identities in the British Television Production of Euro '96', *International Review for the Sociology of Sport*, vol.39, no.4, 2004, pp. 437–55.
2. Ernest Gellner, *Nations and Nationalism*, New York 1983.
3. Alan Bairner, *Sport, Nationalism, and Globalization: European and North American Perspectives*, New York 2001.
4. Bairner, p. xi.
5. Samuel P. Huntington, *Who Are We? The Challenges to America's National Identity*, New York 2005. pp. 21–3.
6. P. W. Preston, *Political/Cultural Identity: Citizens and Nations in a Global*

Era, London 1997.

7   Michael Messner, *Power at Play: Sports and the Problem of Masculinity*, Boston 1992.

8.   Mai Yamani, *Cradle of Islam: The Hijaz and the Quest for an Arabian Identity*, London 2004.

9.   P. R. Kumaraswamy, 'Who Am I? The Identity Crisis in the Middle East', *The Middle East Review of International Affairs, (MERIA)*, vol. 10, no. 1, Article 5, March 2006, available at: http://meria.idc.ac.il/journal/2006/issue1/Kumaraswamy.pdf.

10   James Onley, 'Transnational Merchants in the Nineteenth-Century Gulf: the Case of the Safar Family', in Maadawi Al-Rasheed, Maadawi ed., *Transnational Connections and the Arab Gulf*, London 2004, pp. 59–90.

11. Benedict Anderson, *Imagined Communities: Reflections on the Origin and Spread of Nationalism*, revised edn, London 1991, pp. 5–7.

12. N. Janardhan, 'GCC Countries Evolve Sporting Way to Success', Gulf Research Centre Analysis, 3 December 2006.available at: http://www.arabnews.com/?page=6&section=0&article=89224&d=27&m=11&y=2006.

13. http://www.aspire.qa/intro.htm.

14. Char Simons, 'Doha's Grand Games', *Saudi Aramco World*, March/April 2007, pp. 24–35.

15. John Irish, 'Gulf Investments in Sports, Games Theory', *MEED*, vol. 50, no. 41, 13–19 October 2006 , pp. 4–5 and 27.

16. Janardhan.

17. Simons, p. 28.

18. Simons, p. 31.

19. http://www.doha-2006.com/upload_iis/files/publications/Media_Services%20Guide.pdf.

20. Irish, p. 4.

21. Irish, p. 4.

22. Irish, p. 5.

23. Irish, p. 5.

24. Irish, p. 5.

25. Janardhan.

26. http://www.ameinfo.com/117911.html.

27. Asif Iqbal, The Future of Cricket in Sharjah?Available at: http://www.pakstop.com/pmforums/showthread.php?t=3798.

28. Janardhan.

29. http://www.ocasia.org/ba_games.asp.

30. Paul Dresch, 'Societies, Identities and Global Issues', in Paul Dresch and James Piscatori eds, *Monarchies and Nations: Globalisation and Identity in the Arab States of the Gulf*, London, 2005. p. 3.

31. Simons, p. 26.

32. Francis Fukuyama, 'Identity and Migration', *Prospect*, February 2007, pp. 26–31.
33 F. Gregory Gause, III, *Oil Monarchies Domestic and Security Challenges in the Arab Gulf States*, New York 1994.
34. See: http://www.tourismireland.com/corporate/news/index.cfm/level/category/aID/336/type/Category/subpage/details/id/137.
35. Fukuyama, p. 31.
36. Janardhan.
37. 'Serious Work and Play for Gulf Monarchies' Elite Youth', *Gulf States Newsletter*, vol. 31, issue 797, 9 January 2007, pp. 1–3.
38. Kausik Bandyopadhyay, 'Prologue: The Real People's Game', in *Soccer and Society*, vol. 7, nos 2–3, April–July 2006, pp. 157–64.
39. Bandyopadhyay, p. 157.
40. Chehabi Houchang, 'The Politics of Football in Iran', *Soccer and Society*, vol. 7, nos 2–3, April–July 2006, pp. 223–61.
41. Sam Mchombo, 'Sports and Development in Malawi', *Soccer and Society*, vol. 7, nos 2–3 April–July 2006, pp. 318–38.
42. Amir Ben-Porat, 'Split Loyalty: Football-cum-Nationality in Israel', *Soccer and Society*, vol. 7, nos 2–3, April–July 2006, pp. 262–77.
43. R. Gruneau, 'Making Spectacle: A Case Study in Television Sports Production' in L. Wenner, ed., *Media, Sports and Society*, London 1989, pp. 134–54.
44. Robert Winder, 'The Lost Tribes', *New Statesman*, 21 June 2004. Also available at http://www.newstatesman.com/200406210003; Stephen Tomkins, 'Matches Made in Heaven', *BBC News*, available at:http://newsvote.bbc.co.uk/mpapps/pagetools/print/news.bbc.co.uk/2/hi/uk_news/magazine/3828767.stm.
45. Charlotte Speechly, 'Football – A New Religion?'. See http://arsenal.live-football.co.uk/newsarticle.asp?article=530.
46. Simons, p. 30.
47. See http://www.soccerway.com/news/2007/January/27/kuwaitis-protest-for-change-after-gulf-cup-debacle/; also see http://www.weyak.ae/channels/news/english/?q=node/621596
48. http://archive.gulfnews.com/indepth/gulfcup2007/more_stories/10101558.html.
49. http://archive.gulfnews.com/indepth/gulfcup2007/more_stories/10101556.html.
50. http://archive.gulfnews.com/indepth/gulfcup2007/more_stories/10101556.html.
51. http://www.gia.gov.ae/giawebsite/english/news/content/index.asp?news_id=1009.
52. http://archive.gulfnews.com/indepth/gulfcup2007/more_stories/10101558.html.

53.   http://archive.gulfnews.com/indepth/gulfcup2007/more_stories/10101558.
       html.
54.   http://archive.gulfnews.com/indepth/gulfcup2007/more_stories/10101558.
       html.

SEVEN

Media as Social Matrix in the United Arab Emirates

Nada Mourtada-Sabbah, Mohammed al-Mutawa,
John W. Fox and Tim Walters

Seas of Change and Gulfs between Generations

Within only decades, the United Arab Emirates has witnessed a tidal wave of economic, social and ideological change. In comparison to change experienced elsewhere in the world from globalisation, the wave could be likened to a tsunami. The flickering images on the screen have been part and parcel of the new physical infrastructure that has created an electronic world, engulfing these once tribal peoples. While much has been said about the new economies of scale in products imported, skyscrapers erected, and traditional lineages overseeing corporations,[1] little has been said about the impact of imported media upon the cosmology of the indigenous Emiratis. Yet, a market economy armed with sophisticated media ceaselessly bombards the citizens and expatriate workers alike with messages of consumer (and secular) behaviour. Very few people can ignore the visual images seductively enacting life dramas before them.[2]

Do the electronic media – and especially television, the Internet, and film – constitute the new all-encompassing social matrix for socialising the young of the UAE to value consumption above most other pursuits? If so, then the media would have replaced the extended family as the main source of values and the source for understanding about the world in which they live.

Peers of one's children who are also exposed to the same imagery thus become surrogates for grandparents, parents, and aunts and uncles in approving or disapproving of ideals of how to comport oneself in building social relationships. As such, the bedrock of Emirati society has experienced a seismic shift. And the values that are transmitted by the media relate to the material world of status and the lifestyle of leisure, rather than the duties within an extended kinship network as specified under Islam. The social code of Islam was crafted to fit the social fabric of Bedouin and town-dwelling merchants and craftsmen. The media thus present a sudden challenge to the foundation of society.

The coming-of-age Emiratis transmit new information they gain through education, through conventional media and through interaction on the Internet. These offspring buy designer clothing, French perfume and brand-name accessories. They have abandoned not only the bare cobblestones of the humid and non-air-conditioned souk for the comfort of the modern mall, but many may well have forsaken the culture of their forebears only two generations removed. They have abandoned the Bedouin virtues of self-sufficiency, localised culture, thrift, and social bonds of tribe and family.[3] Today, new loyalties are increasingly likely to go to material possessions.

Already recognising the need to syncretise global and local culture, one Dubai-based television station has departed from standard, mundane Arabic fare and stiff news programming to present 'quality' family entertainment. It hopes to capture an audience already favourably hooked on Westernised entertainment fare, based on audience surveys which suggest that people prefer Western content. In creating this business model, Channel One Television, a twenty-four-hour free satellite service, imports programming from Fox, Disney, Columbia and Warner Brothers.[4]

Channel One has a new policy not to broadcast programmes that may 'offend culturally, religiously, or socially'.[5] Even so, such entertainment is by nature mind-changing. While their shows do not offend directly, they present role models of life and lifestyle. They show clothing styles worn by attractive models or actors. They show material goods possessed by the actors as symbols of the successful life, and one clearly meant to be emulated by the viewers. They also show secularism. Put together in slick, seductive and memorable packaging, they are 'sticky' because they adhere to the consciousness or subconsciousness of the viewer.[6] That the lifestyles and goods are used by actors whom the viewers find appealing is a powerful inducement to emulate them. The content of programmes such as *Friends*, *Extreme Makeover* and *Survivor* illustrate the subtlety of the 'hook' in penetrating the minds of the regular viewers.[7]

The remainder of this chapter examines what we consider to be the magnitude of the socialisation by media in penetrating the cultural fabric of the UAE.

From Tents to Condos: Let There Be a PC and TV for Everyone

The rising knowledge-driven economy of the UAE both depends upon modern media to accomplish its goals and interacts with that media to create a new, distinctly Gulf cosmology. As a result of this new people-media amalgamation, Emirati culture has been affected because examples for life have become intertwined with electronic habits of a new 'life literacy'. This 'new wave'[8] has revolutionised the imagery in the Middle East, and appears to contrast with what religious values have defined as ideal personal conduct. The traditional culture of the Bedouin, codified in the Qur'an and *hadiths*, extols the values of honour, prudence, goodwill, nobility, wisdom, gentleness, justice, control, good sense and dignity. Leaders were especially admired for displaying patience, hospitality, responsibility, honour, honesty and bravery.[9]

The general population has moved from kinship-based neighbour-hoods (the *freij*),[10] to high-rise apartments or suburban villas that are walled off from the neighbours. Cities such as Abu Dhabi and Dubai have populations of more than a million each, whose citizens live increasingly impersonal lives. The nuclear family, perhaps with grand-parents, represents the basic residential social unit. Outlying emirates such as Umm Al Quain and Fujairah are now threatened with slow depopulation as their younger citizens relocate to these larger urban areas for greater economic opportunity. Sharjah has become to some degree a dwelling community for people who work in Dubai. Dubai now houses offices for a majority of the Fortune 500 companies.

Within the past year, Ras al Khaimah has gone from being an isolated backwater located near the tip of the Horn of Arabia to building a state-of-the-art planned city within a perfect square along a canal dredged from the Straits of Hormuz. Architects have thrown the modernist manual for the building out of the window and have designed some to resemble giant flying carpets and other images from *The Thousand and One Nights* (or simply the 'Arabian Nights'). Dubai has a much-deserved reputation for the architectural sublime, ranging from manmade islands in the shape of the world to the tallest building in the world. Together, a surreal sense of almost virtuality pervades the built environment for this first generation of urban pioneers in the three major cities of the emirates. Their architecture reflects a virtuality of a life lived in front of the flickering images from the broadcast media, and a blending of the technologies from the West with images from the Middle East.

Individualism and Status

Virtually the entire native population has become urbanised even though the former mainstay of the traditional economy – the herding of Emirati-owned camels by workers from the subcontinent – con-tinues in the vast stretches of the lightly populated interior. What remains of the date groves along the coasts and around oases is tended by expatriate labour. Most of the nationals maintain homes within the capital city of their emirate, as well as often on their outlying ancestral lands. Life within the built urban environs of concrete and glass has radically changed the nature of social relationships. It also changes the basic way in which nature is perceived.

Jobs have changed from the type performed by several members of the family and tribe working together in close association to the type held by a single person working within a large corporation in the private sector or an agency or bureau within the public sector. As Emiratis have relocated to the city, money has become increasingly important; families do not produce themselves the things they need as they did in pastoralism, arboriculture (date farming) or fishing. In short, the traditional life on the desert sands, in oases and in some coastal fishing villages has been radically transformed to market exchange.[11] Money is the currency, increasingly more now than family relationships with their accompanying expectations of favours owed. Such a dramatic metamorphosis naturally reduces the importance of face-to-face relationships within the tribe and how religious values are perceived. Formerly, Islam and the time-honoured ways of the ancestors were the sole source of authority of ideas. Now authority also arrives via the airwaves in what the international market can convey.

Not surprisingly, recent survey data show that college-educated Emiratis under the age of twenty-five are significantly more secular and individualistic than their older siblings or parents within a cohort of greater than twenty-five years of age.[12] This key age span of a quarter of a century approximates the duration of prevalent television viewing within the UAE. This time interval thus speaks to different perceptual worlds experienced by the two generational cohorts.

To contrast some dimensions of the two different worlds experienced by the respective cohorts, life within tribalism/collectivism emphasises 'we', not the more hedonistic 'I'. Group life also promotes interdependence, in-group harmony and collaboration. Group goals and internal harmony are more highly valued over those from outside the group. Individuals extraneous to the tribal group may even be represented as perennial enemies and rivals for the exploitation of local resources (for example, herding lands, fishing rights). Most of all, there is a sense of collective identity that carries with it a sense of honour and duty to defend members of one's extended group and usually to put their interests over those of oneself.

In contrast, the younger Emiratis display more of the individual-ism characteristic of the West. It seems odd that youngsters in Dubai and in New York have more in common than either group does with their grandparents' generation. In the case of the young cohort, the importance of the individual seems to be increasingly valued over the group. He/she makes individual choices in the selection of products to consume. Rather than the informal law of the tribe, much of the formal law has recently come to encode the rights of the individuals to rights over his/her private property, and to some freedom of expres-sion. In sum, an individualistic society uses the pronoun 'I', stressing individual goals and individuals who manage their own affairs so that the individual may be increasingly self-actualised through work and lifestyle choices.

The media marketplace is the source of the goods upholding the new Emirati identity of the individual. The market furnishes advertis-ing, entertainment and news, which together comprise many of the ideas that are used by individuals to evaluate their purchases. Prodded by all these media messages, the young generation seem to be develop-ing a 'secular consumer religion' as a counterpart to the traditional values of group life encoded in Islam. Advertising campaigns and entertainment implicitly question the values and practices undergird-ing traditional notions of how the individual should submit to the desired duties and obligations among kindred and neighbours.

The political scientist Benjamin Barber, in his *Jihad vs. McWorld*, noted the impact of information coupled with entertainment, which is termed infotainment. In Barber's dichotomy, *jihad* represents local culture galvanised against the intrusive global technology, pop culture and integrated markets. In contrast to the local traditional culture, McWorld relates to 'onrushing economic technological and ecological forces that demand integration and uniformity and that mesmerize peoples everywhere with fast music, fast computers and fast food ... pressing nations into one homogenous global theme park, one McWorld tied together by communications, information, entertainment, and commerce'.[13] In a matter of several years, the regular internalising of messages through both advertising and attempting to emulate the scenes of actors creating a lifelike situation can create a new collective mental structure of how life should be lived for an autonomous population.

If so, then advertising and sitcoms have contributed substantially to a new Emirati ideal. This prototype locates needs in conspicuous consumption rather than in 'content of work' or in meeting the needs of the less fortunate if one already has enough material goods, which is an axiom of Islam. The point is that one can never have enough if prodded by images that indicate that the sky is the limit. This value of unlimited good is abetted by the sudden and enormous oil revenues. As conspicuous consumption becomes the ideal, the marketplace of material goods replaces ideals inherited from generations past as the place where the new culture is experienced first hand. And as commercial art comes to represent perceived reality, advertising becomes a replacement metaphor for life experienced.

Even their memory webs (group-based memories defining life) have been hardwired in a different way from those of their parents.[14] The social matrix in which the young generation understands the meaning of information is dissimilar to that of their parents, as is their sense of collective memory.[15] Technology such as the Internet, with its power to create different associations, and the mobile phone have catalysed this process. So, too, has post-secondary education. These children not only process information differently from their parents, but they also create different communities with which they surround themselves.[16] Higher education was not part of the Emirati experience until very recently. At the time of independence, there were only two university graduates within the entire country.

The effects of the media on one's concept of self are profound. Advertising, for example, channels the desire to shape oneself in the depicted mode of desirable behaviour – such as riding a polo pony or sailing a yacht. People can thus assemble themselves to ameliorate social and personal frustration while creating new habits and identities. A total makeover is even possible through acquiring the necessary symbols. On the personal level, if you don't feel acceptable, all you need to do is purchase something to make you look and feel more like the projected ideal of the successful person. And if that doesn't momentarily satiate the void in personal fulfilment, then one can simply buy a powerful automobile to complete the makeover. Young people in the UAE do drive an inordinately high number of the latest models of Mercedes, Lexuses and other luxury cars.

The marketplace, then, is not merely a metaphor about diverse ideas coming together, as in universities, but has the more literal meaning of a locus of purchasing what may be perceived as needed for the creation of individualistic identities. Of course, the new identities really are not individualistic because they are contrived through advertising. In the UAE, as elsewhere in the world market, consumption is becoming an acceptable means of acting out fantasies. Movies and television offer an escape from the drudgery of life on the job, outside of the warm and enduring relationships of the extended family, in a cinematographic fantasy existence. Clothing and accessories become symbols bespeaking social values and success. A commonly told joke suggests that man is judged by three things – his car, his mobile and his suit. For a man, the car can be nothing less than a BMW or Mercedes, the mobile is the 167-gram, 'styled for life' Nokia 9300,[17] and the suit must be Armani. As a point of contrast, it is still within memory that the father of this man was judged solely by his honour in upholding the value of his lineage name. The lineage name also indicated who his kinsmen were if the man was wronged, and who would avenge any misdeeds done to this individual if the value of the family honour was breached in any way.

Roles of the New Emirati Family

As we have seen, consumerism carries a distinct worldview of what to dream for to live the good life. The overt consumerism inherent in advertising and the more subtle influence in entertainment continue to impact on the perception of what Emirati family life should be. Because adopting a 'proper' lifestyle is part of a desire to fit in, a lingering danger is that local customs could become objects of derision or rejection, especially among the young Emiratis. However, there still remains a strong value in respecting the older generation. The internal conflict between new and old does not seem to lead to the degrees of psychological conflict found in other parts of the world. Rather, compartmentalisation allows Arab values, language and cosmology to be used within the home, and the global worldview, its accompanying values and the English language, to be used in business and education, or what would be considered as the public sphere.[18]

Lamenting what he believes is the lessening of Arab culture in the public sphere, one passionate observer offered the following opinion in the *Gulf News* (Dubai):

> ... As an Arab parent ... I fear that each of my two sons is growing into a person and a half ... instead of two persons. Each is a full-fledged global child and a distorted resemblance of an Arab child. ... I would like each one to be two-persons in one, with the Arab person in them being the more paramount...[19]

The government hopes to develop both such 'persons', because an educated, skilled and informed workforce will provide the human capital to fuel intelligent growth. If this new marketplace of goods and ideas is where the Emirati world is headed, then fundamental values dear to tribal society are in jeopardy,[20] and are now rendered to second-class status suitable for the home only. This is because developed (educated) human capital almost always creates a sense of personal responsibility.[21] Such an individual is almost invariably linked to a market imperative model – a model that will, if it continues unabated, force change.[22]

Within the newly formed urban centres, nuclear family homes (called villas) are spread out in suburban subdivisions. The villa usually has a wall surrounding it, more typical of Middle Eastern spatial propriety, rather than the open front lawn leading directly to the windows of the house, as in the West, for all to see. In polygamous households, there may be as many as three or four separate houses, although all are usually built in the same style, within the single walled-off family compound.

The Emirati palate seems to have gone chic in one short generation; the young are wont to eat typical fast foods found in the West, and the parents have a wide variety of international restaurants to choose from. Prepared foods have replaced home-cooked ones, although there are often domestic servants (from the subcontinent) who may cook. Diets clearly have changed, with a wide variety of international foods also available in the supermarkets. Families typically spend less time gathered together around the supper table. Entertainment during or following the meal has become less of a shared social experience in places such as the communal *majlis* and more of a choice of individuals.[23]

Most revolutionary of all is that adolescent or unmarried women typically venture out in public, either by themselves or preferably with several mates (of the same gender) of their own age, and go to places such as the mall, a movie or a restaurant. In fact, the gathering spot for young singles is often an American chain restaurant. On Thursday (the beginning of the weekend), groups of four or five females, clad in typical black *abayas*, can often be seen conversing with one another while eating an American meal such as a hamburger, French fries and coleslaw.

The role of both parents has also dramatically changed. The father's role has shifted from that of a patriarch, overseeing the labour of his adult sons who might have once been involved in a family-managed activity such as herding camels or goats (perhaps with one's cousins), to the role of a wage earner or manager of a family business (even if it is run by expatriates). While the father remains the titular head of the household and is accorded much respect, he no longer commands the same absolute authority as in the past.

A typical mother now directs the family's activities of consumption, rather than preparing the meals herself (for example, various porridges of mashed dates and their extracts). No longer the repository of crafts, such as baskets and mats woven from palm leaves, she now chooses from a wide plethora of imported goods that her family will consume. Such also redirects what it means to be a woman and the key values accompanying that meaning.[24] More than likely she will be involved in arranging the marriages of her offspring – ideally, although less probably, with cousins. A mate from the family circle of friends would be more likely now. From a rational choice perspective, it should be kept in mind that a marriage requires a substantial outlay of cash for the bride *mahr*, which not infrequently amounts to $100,000. The groom gives the money to the bride for her to keep. New considerations have arisen in marriage choices, such as degrees of education and the likelihood of fewer numbers of betrothals per person (with a statistical trend towards monogamy). The more highly educated the bride, the larger the bride *mahr*. Finally, increased education unwittingly functions as a form of birth control, since the age of first marriage (and consequently first birth) has risen from about seventeen to twenty-three for women.[25] Despite what the government publicly promotes as desirable, typical family size is dropping. The women studied by Walters come from families of about eight children; their older cousins have about six children. They want families with still fewer offspring.[26]

The role and status of women are in a state of flux. While Emirati women rarely work in the private sector, less well-off women may work in the public sector in a myriad of governmental positions. This ratio of women working outside the home will accelerate when the present generation graduates from university. Women account for some 80 percent of university graduates within the UAE. Not only have they been trained in data-processing skills so necessary for an informational economy, but they have also been socialised as conspicuous consumers of brand names. Their education allows them greater understandings of the wide range of goods that may be acquired from the world at large. Female students from local universities are said to disappear not infrequently from class for three or four days; the instructor may eventually find out that they simply went to Paris on a shopping spree for a major forthcoming event, such as the wedding of a sibling, which requires particularly elegant attire.

A poster recently displayed at a cafeteria at a women's university in Abu Dhabi epitomises the conflicting crosscurrents of change for women in ascertaining what paths they will personally follow. The poster was provocatively titled, 'What kinda girl r u?' Underneath the headline, the student who created the poster wrote the following lament, which seems to summarise the problems within a highly dynamic transition from traditionalism to globalisation and the accompanying pressures to conform to a new ideal like that presented in the media.

> *Are local women more materialistic?*
> Of course we are. Look at how much we own in contrast to our grandparents, who led perfectly happy lives not so long ago. Take a look around you. I think you will be able to spot all of the Dior handbags released from the latest collection. Do you think such lifestyles are sustainable? Not in the long term, unless your family name is bint Bill Al-Gates [sic]. [27]
>
> People continuously grumble over how the local men are marrying foreigners. Did anybody ask why such a trend is emerging? In most cases, it is because they wouldn't be able to afford supporting such extravagant lifestyles. Do you have to been [sic] seen wearing an outfit for a limited number of times only? Does that

imply a lack of self-confidence and hence a weakness in character?

Change must come from within, so next time you go shopping, ask yourself these questions:

How desperately do I need this?

How often do I plan on using it?

The last time I bought one, how much use did I get out of it?

This time, will I be able to make better use of it?

Or

Can I make do without it?

Emirati women thus find themselves in a spiralling vortex in which they gravitate to ever-escalating consumerist habits, which in turn are putting strains on the earlier customs of marriage, forcing women out of the household into employment. The taste for the chic and exotic thus is steadily undermining the traditional anchor role of marriage and raising children.

Shopping Knows No Limit

Shopping infrastructure in the UAE is a major factor in the changing roles and expectations of Emirati women. The 'shop-till-you-drop' ethic is developed in the UAE as a special niche to entice shoppers from the nearby Gulf states, as well as those from Central Asia and Europe. Russians find the retail shopping so lucrative that thousands of entrepreneurs make a full-time living by purchasing luxury goods inexpensively in Dubai and selling them for substantial profits in Moscow.

Shopping is coupled with tourist sights. Dubai has led the way in building eye-catching attractions, such as the world's tallest buildings, manmade islands in the shape of palm trees and even an indoor snow-ski slope. However, Dubai is one of the most oil deficient of the Gulf emirates. Because of this, hardly a week passes without a mega-development plan being announced to keep the cash registers humming with tourist purchases.[28] While Dubai provided 17 percent of retail footage in the six Gulf Cooperation Council countries in 2004, the expectation is that Dubai will offer 30 percent of all Gulf retail space within five years.[29] This is a monumental marker because Dubai presently ranks third in the world in per capita retail space, just after the US and Singapore.[30] Because Dubai plans to attract 15 million tourists yearly by 2010, the existing 27 million square feet of shopping space in Dubai is a sound foundation for a niche that will continue to be enhanced.[31]

Sotheby's and Christie's, the two premier auction houses for the fine arts, report that the Dubai market ranks third in the purchase of world-class art. The Emirati elite are decorating their spacious villas mostly with Western antiques, and the vast white walls with Western paintings. In the past, the walls would have been left blank. The Emiratis have acquired a taste for art only within the past decade. Prior to that, there was such an intensive desire to leave the old and traditional behind, that virtually all of their traditional material culture was exported, mostly as tourist souvenirs. There was a compelling psychological need to acquire the latest in modern technology, and especially so if it was electronic and was showy (especially with luminosity). Emirati tastes have been tempered somewhat for the refined and antiquarian of *haute couture* from elsewhere.

In contrast, the malls offer an exotic shopping experience, so that the shoppers get the feeling of penetrating exotic lands in the quest for treasures to be discovered on one hand and the elegant on the other. American and European luxury stores have locations in Dubai (for example, Tiffany of New York). The exotic and chic are blended in air-conditioned malls that are the new town squares, where Emiratis can see and be seen by their fellow citizens engaged in the widespread pastime of shopping. Recently constructed malls range from a Moroccan bazaar (perhaps modelled on the fabled souk of Marrakech) to a Renaissance Italian town square (aptly named the Mercado) to a mall with three Egyptian-style pyramids comprising the roof, and giant sphinxes and statues of pharaohs at its entrances. Designer labels can be found at discounted prices below those of Paris, London or New York because there are no import duties or sales taxes. Nonetheless, it all is available. Parisian crystal may be purchased in themes that are dear to Emiratis, such as horses or camels.

The luxury items are widely advertised in the local print media. For example, a Sony Plasma television is not only a 'Sign of the Good Life' but should be 'the focus of modern living space'.[32] At 2XL furniture, home has become 'an expression of you the person'.[33] The Nissan Murano not only 'becomes you', but 'is a sculpture in motion'.[34] The Nokia 9300 is both 'Business' and 'Class'.[35] The Citibank Teen Credit Card 'empowers teenagers while giving them responsibility'.[36] The Lexus RX 330 makes 'everyday life exhilarating'. You can 'wear a statement' when you put on Westar Wrist fashion.[37] The Max New Spring Collection lets you 'look good' and 'feel good'.[38] The artwork accompanying these print ads shows a modern, Westernised vision of today's 'smart' Emirati surrounded by his or her possessions.

The need for continual profits further pressures the retail sector to try new ploys in advertising to bring in local shoppers to supplement those from abroad. Increases in sensationalism, personal drama and trivialisation are found in the advertising. The most frequently watched shows in the Emirates also speak to the same trends of sensationalism and trivialisation. Standard television fare ranges from *telenovellas* and soap operas to American movies and sitcoms. The lowering of the boundaries among news, entertainment, drama and advertising creates analytical frames for looking at the day's issues.

You Are What You Watch on Television

Over time, demonstrations of how life should be lived buried in entertainment can have powerful effects. Not only can these help shape impressions about which options should dominate, they can help create a common vision around a central organising idea for life. Many studies clearly support the generalisation that much 'learning' takes place through observing the dramatised behaviour of others on television.[39]

It has long been known that propaganda should evoke an audience's interest, must be transmitted through an attention-getting communications medium, and should label events and people with distinctive phrases or slogans.[40] If these ring familiar, it is because they form the operating rationale for entertainment and advertising packages. They help create 'sticky' (memorable and difference-making) messages.[41] These packages are now beamed via satellite into and through traditional land transmitters across the United Arab Emirates.

Entertainment teaches anti-traditional behaviours from subliminal meanings crafted into the programming. Some youth contend that their friends should watch television that is purposefully against traditional values to show their independence from traditional manifestations of authority. Some of this programming is so overtly provocative that even the older siblings by just five years or so feel that younger brothers and sisters should not be exposed to it.[42] And, because many modern Emirati houses feature single-person bedrooms secluded from parents, these youngsters view these programmes in private.[43] More than occasionally, females are portrayed as lusty, scantily clothed (by Islamic standards), and may even undulate their hips to the beat of music in video clips. Featured on Arabic networks such as Rotana TV, which specialises in Arabic music video clips, concerts, festivals and musical programmes, these images arrive in their bedrooms via satellite and the Internet.[44] Surely they have an impact on young women, who may experience confusion with the expectations for traditional gender roles.

Make no mistake about it, the Emirati youth overwhelming prefer Western entertainment – either feature-length movies or shows on comedy channels, such as *Friends*, *Who Will Win a Million* or *Mad*

About You. They watch a Telemundo programme called *Rosalindo* and a popular Egyptian serial about a husband with four wives. While soap operas are viewed because they deal with the conflicts of basic family human relationships, they typically show women at home unveiled. Young females also watch women's-issue programming about marriage, divorce, family, children and fashion.[45]

Such lifestyle advocacy may touch upon sensitive religious and political subjects. Because of the seductive power of media, a subversive anti-traditional bias in programming has become a quiet and occasionally not-so-quiet political and societal issue. It is not discussed much in newspapers, but it does on occasion creep into Friday morning sermons at mosques around the emirates. The line of reasoning is that we cannot just embrace part of the Western package that is projected as globalisation. A recent Parents Television Council study of American primetime television suggested that entertainment programming tended to depict religion negatively.[46]

Trends of Changes Compounded into a Grand Disjunction

What is happening in today's United Arab Emirates is an Arab parallel to the American societal rift Ewen chronicled in *Captains of Consciousness* and *Channels of Desire*. Policy, infrastructure, education, literacy and marketplace are all converging into a postmodern global society geared to the world economy.[47] Whether the resulting wind of change ultimately blows ill or good depends upon several factors. For one, global capitalism invokes individualism and the driving force of the marketplace, along with increased education and informational transparency.[48] A whole generation of young men and women must integrate the world of their parents with the unrelenting demands of work to generate profit amid competition and the uncertainties of job insecurity.[49]

The educational requisite for an informational economy has already created a generational schism among Emiratis. Education has come in many forms, from schoolbooks to travel to a mediated environment presenting worlds of possibilities. Urbane and educated women consider themselves more ambitious, more secular, more independent and more capable than do their less educated, rural sisters.[50] Regardless of gender, the more educated believe that an exciting life, equality and a sense of accomplishment are personally important. Those who are less educated believe that loyalty and harmony are the most important personal qualities.[51]

Society might already have reached a threshold of no return in the cumulative trends in the movement toward globalisation. Analogous to Wilson and Kelling's 'Broken Windows Theory', the UAE's open windows might well be creating the context for inexorable and inevitable alteration.[52] What this means is that accumulation of a few relatively minor changes in viewing habits, purchasing patterns and life outlook, creates a springboard for more profound societal shifts. These shifts are already well under way with a younger, well-educated generation who are aspiring to different lifestyles from those of their parents.

A continuing compartmentalisation of the two sets of coexisting ways of life – the global life with its information-driven economy, its control and its value to the marketplace, versus the local life based on Bedouin-derived traditions – is particularly difficult to reconcile. On the one hand, the ruler of Dubai has advocated an open debate of all issues; on the other, the Dubai police chief says he will take off the air television channels that violate cultural norms.[53] These different viewpoints suggest that Emirati leaders are still searching for a practical middle way to incorporate local standards and orientations into a globally viable synthesis. The United Arab Emirates hopes to catapult into the future without pain, but this may be difficult to achieve. Clearly, this in-between generation in their early twenties face the hurdle of adopting the best that modern technology offers while retaining key aspects of traditional culture. Some argue that the steady advent of technology makes the evolution toward markets and their ideas inevitable.[54] Whether Emiratis are able to mesh the effects of a media matrix with their traditional core values, such as religion and family, will determine the nation's social stability.

Notes

1. John W. Fox, Nada Mourtada-Sabbah, and Mohammed al-Mutawa, 'The Arab Gulf Region: Traditionalism Globalized or Globalization Traditionalized?', in *Globalization and the Gulf*, John W. Fox, Nada Mourtada-Sabbah and Mohammed al-Mutawa eds, London 2006, pp. 3–59.

2. Media Awareness Network, 'Music Videos', retrieved 1 May 2004, from http://www.media-awareness.ca/english/parents/music, n.d.

3. T. Walters, S. Quinn and A. Jendli, 'Media, Culture, and Society: The Roadmap to Life', Modernization, Globalization, and Cross-Cultural Communication, The Tenth International Conference on Cross-Cultural Communication, Taipei, Taiwan, July 2005.

4. Available films are the likes of *Harry Potter*, *Lord of the Rings* and *The Matrix*. Series include *Extreme Makeover*, *American Idol*, *Survivor*, *Friends* and *Frasier*.

5. B. Za`Za', 'New TV Channel To Provide Latest Entertainment', *Gulf News*, 23 December 2004, p. 5.

6. M. Gladwell, *The Tipping Point*, New York 2002.

7. '*Friends* focuses on three men and three women in their thirties as they pursue career and personal success in Manhattan. Monica is a chef obsessed with neatness and order. Her brother, Ross, has a more complicated life, with three failed marriages and a crush on Monica's best friend, Rachel. Rounding out the cast are Monica's husband, Chandler, the ever-clueless Joey, and the quirky Phoebe. PTC considered *Friends* one of the raciest sitcoms in primetime because all six regulars have been sexually active, and dialogue contains vulgar language and explicitly sexual content. In past episodes, sexual promiscuity, Monica's endorsement of Chandler's fondness for porn, and Joey's many, many sexual partners has served as joke fodder. Also Rachel gave birth to Ross's child, the result of an alcoholic induced one-night stand.' Parents Television Council, 'Family TV Guide, *Friends*', http://www.parentstv.org/ptc/shows/main.asp?shwid=568, n.d.; IMDb, Plot summary for *Friends*, http://www.imdb.com/title/tt0108778/plotsummary, n.d.

 'Each episode of *Extreme Makeover* features two individuals seeking drastic changes to their appearance. Unhappy with their features, weight, or general appearance, they are treated to several procedures, including plastic surgery. Episodes have featured graphic scenes of surgical operations and anatomical references, particularly involving women's breasts. The series has also contained blurred nudity, showing breasts prior to augmentation. The extreme measures people go to in order to change their natural appearance conveys a negative message to viewers regarding self-worth and self-esteem.' Parents Television Council, 'Family TV Guide, *Extreme Makeover*', http://www.parentstv.org/ptc/shows/main.asp?shwid=1678, n.d.

'Past seasons of *Survivor* have featured people screaming obscenities at each other and walking around naked. Late night discussions have included descriptions of sexual exploits. Coupled with lying and backstabbing, the content in *Survivor* usually leaves much to be desired. Each season is a little different, however and the *Survivor: All Stars* welcomed the return of the season one winner, Richard Hatch, who is nude (pixilated) almost constantly. Parents Television Council, 'Family TV Guide, *Survivor*'.

8. In the sense of Alvin Toffler's, *The Third Wave*, New York 1981.
9. S. Swan and T. Walters, 'A People in Transition?', unpublished manuscript, Dubai: Zayed University, 2004.
10. John W. Fox, Nada Mourtada-Sabbah and Mohammed al-Mutawa, 'Heritage Revivalism in Sharjah', in Fox et al., *Globalization,* pp. 266–87.
11. The local slump in the pearl trade in the late 1920s and early 1930s that accompanied the Great Depression brought poverty, distress and insecurity to the 'hardy, religious, individualistic and pragmatic lords of the desert'. By the 1950s, many Bedouin, needing money, sent their men to earn a living in the oilfields in other Gulf states. As a result, many tribesmen spent long periods outside their immediate tribal network, and tribal bonds weakened. Then, in the 1960s, as real oil wealth began to come to the emirates, tribesmen began earning living wages from local oil companies. The easier life of the towns attracted them and their families, and tribal links weakened further still. Simultaneously, rulers found less time to sit in *majlis* with their Bedouin subjects as in the past. As a result, the arm's-length familiarity between the two has been lost, replaced by a new, more emotionally distant form. (J. Walker, 'The Bedu, Towns and Rulers in the Emirates, 1920–1970', in *Bedouin Society in the Emirates*, Center for Documentation and Research, Abu Dhabi, 2005)
12. T. Walters, S. Quinn and A. Jendli, 'Media, Culture, and Society: The Roadmap to Life', Modernization, Globalization, and Cross-Cultural Communication, the Tenth International Conference on Cross-Cultural Communication, Taipei, Taiwan, July 2005.
13. Benjamin R. Barber, *Jihad versus McWorld*, New York 1995.
14. J. Barwind and T. Walters, 'Swimming in the Bio-Cultural Soup: The Cell Phone and Society in the UAE', Theoretical Approaches and Practical Applications, Russian Communication Association, Rostov-na-Donu, 2004; T. Walters and L. Walters, 'The Social Consequences of Media Life Among Students in the UAE', Second International Conference on Communication and Mass Media, Athens Institute for Education and Research, Athens, 2004.

15. J. S. Brown and P. Duguid, *The Social Life of Information*, Boston 2002; D. Wegner, 'Transactive Memory in Close Relationships', *Journal of Personality and Social Disorder* vol. 6, 1991, pp. 923–9.

16. Walters, Quinn and Jendli.

17. Vertu now makes a mobile that has been called a boy's toy. With models costing between Dh17,600 (approximately $4,800) and Dh125,000 (approximately $34,000), these luxury telephones should only sell to celebrities. A local spokesman for Vertu notes that 'a mobile phone has now become an object that people are emotionally attached to and the luxury mobile phone basically takes that attachment a step further by making it a status symbol, similar to a watch or a car.' (V. Bharadwaj, 'It's Essentially a Boy's Toy', *Gulf News*, *Tabloid* section, 10 March 2005, p. 2.)

18. Nada Mourtada-Sabbah, John W. Fox and Mohammed al-Mutawa 'Le syncrétisme entre capitalisme et traditionalisme dans le Golfe arabe', in *Le Golfe Arabique entre Capitalisme et Tradition*; Nada Mourtada-Sabbah, John W. Fox and Mohammed al-Mutawa, eds, *Maghreb-Machrek*, no. 187, Paris 2006, pp. 7–28.

19. J. H. Fakhreddine, 'Who Needs the Arabic Language?' *Gulf News*, section 1, 23 December 2004, p. 9.

20. Ullman, 1997, p. 87.

21. Walters, 2001, pp. 83–5.

22. Selber and Ghanem.

23. Walters, Quinn and Jendli.

24. S. Ewen and E. Ewen, *Channels of Desire: Mass Images and the Shaping of American Consciousness*, 2nd edition, Minneapolis 1992; A. Appadurai, *Modernity at Large: Cultural Dimensions of Globalization*, Minneapolis 1991.

25. Walters, Quinn, and Walters, 2005.

26. T. Walters, 'Attitudes of Zayed University Students', unpublished manuscript, Dubai 2003.

27. *Bint* is Arabic for 'daughter of'.

28. S. Thomson, 'Dubai – On Target For 100 Million Sq. Ft. GLA', Retail International Surveys', http://www.retailinternational.co.uk/survtwo.htm, 2004.

29. Thomson, 2005.

30. AME Info, 'Expanding the City Centre', http://www.ameinfo.com/cgi-bin/cms/limit_country.cgi?ID=3190;Country=United%20Arab%20Emirates, 2 March 2005.

31. Thompson.

32. *Gulf News*, LCD & Plasma Television Special section, 2 March 2005, p. 8.

33. *Gulf News*, 1 March 2005, p. 4.

34. *Gulf News*, 2 March 2005, p. 20.

35. *Gulf News*, 2 March 2005, p. 35.

36.   *Gulf News*, 2 March 2005, p. 58.

37.   *Gulf News*, 2 March 2005, p. 47.

38.   *Gulf News*, 2 March 2005, p. 47.

39.   A. Bandura, *Social Learning Theory*, New Jersey 1976.

40.   'Joseph Goebbels', http://www.psywarrior.com/Goebbels.html, taken from *Goebbels' Principles of Propaganda* by Leonard W. Doob, published in *Public Opinion and Propaganda; A Book of Readings*, the Society for the Psychological Study of Social Issues, n.d.

41.   M. Gladwell, *The Tipping Point*, New York 2002.

42.   A. Jendli and M. Khalifa, 'Effects of Western-Style Arabic Music Video Clips on Emirati Youth Identity and Culture', International Academy for Media Science Conference, Arab Satellites in a Changing World, Cairo, Egypt, June 2004.

43.   Walters, Quinn and Jendli.

44.   Jendli and Khalifa.

45.   Walters, Quinn, and Jendli.

46.   Parents Television Council, n.d. See also Parents Television Council, 1 February 2005; see Gladwell.

47.   Holloway and Dolan, 2002.

48.   'Arab Liberalism and Democracy in the Middle East', *Middle East Review of International Affairs* vol. 8, no. 4, 2004, pp. 20–32.

49.   See Ewen and Ewen.

50.   J. Whiteoak, N. G. Crawford and R. H. Mapstone, *Work Values and Attitudes in an Arab Culture*, Dubai 2004; Walters, 'Attitudes'.

51.   Swan and Walters.

52.   Gladwell; see also J. W. Wilson and G. L. Kelling, 'Broken Windows: The Police and Neighborhood Safety', *The Atlantic Monthly*, vol. 269, no. 3, 1982.

53.   See, for example, M. Stent, 'Be Bold in Tackling Issues, Mohammed Tells Media'. *Gulf News*, 10 January 2005, p. 1; and M. Stent, 'Confines of Law Must Be Eliminated', *Gulf News*, 10 January 2005, p. 1.

54.   H. Y. Amin, 'Social Engineering: Transnational Broadcasting and its Impact on Peace in the Middle East', *Global Media Journal*, vol. 2, no. 4, 2004.

EIGHT

Diversification in Abu Dhabi and Dubai: The Impact on National Identity and the Ruling Bargain

Christopher Davidson

This chapter will reveal the divergent economic development paths of the two wealthiest and most populous members of the United Arab Emirates – Abu Dhabi and Dubai – and will discuss the varying impact of these paths on national identity and political stability. In particular it will be demonstrated that differing historical experiences combined with external events and a vast disparity in oil wealth have led to distinct macroeconomic strategies emerging within an extremely flexible federal state. Despite superficial diversification, oil-rich Abu Dhabi is able to rely on overseas investments and uses its comparative advantage of cheap energy to set up heavy, export-oriented industries, while relatively oil-scarce Dubai has been forced to diversify more rapidly, requiring the emirate to engage higher-risk strategies aimed at courting much greater levels of foreign direct investment. Most notably these have included the promotion of tourism, the establishment of economic 'free zones', and the relaxation of property laws for foreigners. Finally, it will be suggested that the strategies associated with this latter path, if unchecked, may undermine the carefully constructed national identity in Dubai, and thereby weaken certain key components of that emirate's particular brand of monarchical ruling bargain.

Why Do Abu Dhabi and Dubai Have Different Economic Development Paths?

Dubai, as a nineteenth-century breakaway settlement from the sheikhdom of Abu Dhabi, never possessed an agricultural hinterland, yet did possess a natural water inlet, and was governed by a ruling family that embraced free trade and positioned Dubai as a free port in the lower Gulf. Throughout the twentieth century, Dubai's free port status attracted regular influxes of disgruntled merchants from other nearby ports, as taxes were raised, infrastructure crumbled, or persecution was faced. These merchants, including Iranians and Arabistanis, in addition to merchants from the less business-friendly neighbouring sheikhdoms including Abu Dhabi and Sharjah, brought with them valuable business connections and entrepreneurial skills.[1]

Since the 1960s, these key historical differences have been compounded by a huge disparity in oil wealth, or more specifically potential oil wealth, between Abu Dhabi and Dubai. Although the UAE commands nearly 10 percent of the world's proven oil reserves, Abu Dhabi accounts for over 90 percent of the UAE's oil exports, a figure that is growing. Dubai's oil reserves are depleted, with its oil industry gradually winding down. Indeed, while GDP per capita for the UAE is now around $25,000, if one considers the population of UAE nationals and excludes the millions of expatriates, it could be around $75,000. Tellingly, for Abu Dhabi nationals the figure could be as high as $275,000. Dubai does not have the same safety net.[2]

Abu Dhabi's Low-Risk Strategy

Much of Abu Dhabi's oil wealth has been channelled into overseas investments, which began *en masse* in the early 1970s, and must still be regarded as the capstone of the emirate's long-term economic strategy, as the emirate attempts to channel a large proportion of its surplus oil wealth into building a substantial buffer of overseas interest payments that can be called upon to stabilise the domestic economy should there be future oil price slumps or other such periods of austerity. In most cases, the government's investment portfolios are managed by the Abu Dhabi Investment Authority (ADIA), and in many ways the authority's towering new headquarters in the middle of the city's showpiece Corniche Road can be seen as symbolising the centrality of its mission to the local administration.[3] A powerful institution staffed by teams of foreign experts, ADIA scours the globe for a variety of investment opportunities, currently favouring a mixture of 60 percent 'safe bets' in the developed world (such as the recent acquisition of a 5 percent stake in the Fiat-controlled Ferrari[4]), with around 35 percent being focused on the emerging markets of Southeast Asia,[5] and with a few 'wild cards' in areas identified for substantial future growth (such as Libya's tourist infrastructure).[6]

Alongside this financial strategy, Abu Dhabi's oil wealth has been harnessed in an effort to build an internationally competitive industrial base, as the planners have sought to utilise the emirate's abundant cheap energy sources for the purposes of comparative advantage. In most cases the investments selected have been heavy industries geared to the export of metal and plastic-based products that can undercut their oil-importing German and Japanese rivals. Prominent examples would include the Abu Dhabi Polymers Company (also known as Borouge), the Abu Dhabi National Oil Company's partner chemicals firm, Borealis,[7] and the Abu Dhabi Shipbuilding Company, which provides materials for and builds an increasing number of military and commercial vessels.[8] Such a commitment to heavy, large-scale industries can be confirmed by considering the distribution of manufacturing establishments in the UAE: given that Abu Dhabi accounts for much more than half of the country's total manufacturing output, it is highly indicative that the emirate hosts only 224 plants, a mere

10 percent of the total number in the UAE, compared with 817 in Dubai, 716 in Sharjah and 316 in 'Ajman.[9]

Dubai's High-Risk Strategy

Without the oil advantage, Dubai's industries (with the exception of its aluminium export capabilities[10]) have been much lighter and smaller-scale, primarily geared to the production of goods that would otherwise be costly and inefficient to import. Examples of such import-substitution industrialisation would include Dubai's many construction goods manufacturers, which produce bulky items including piping and cement,[11] Dubai's packaging and bottling plants, and the emirate's plethora of basic textiles manufacturers.[12]

With regard to commerce, Dubai has made full use of its described ongoing attractiveness as one the region's premier entrepôts. Indeed, its ports have become some of the busiest in the world, shifting over 15 million metric tonnes of non-oil-related traded goods per year, and accounting for nearly $31 billion in trade receipts per year (compared with just $2 billion in 1975).[13] Boosting trade further, the emirate hosts two major shopping festivals each year, 'The Dubai Shopping Festival', which runs from January to February and is targeted at international buyers, and the 'Dubai Summer Surprises Festival', which runs from July to August and is targeted at visiting GCC buyers. Most famously, of course, Dubai's enormous commercial expansion has transformed it into a city of shopping malls, with some of the largest in the world and with many catering for the highest possible end of the international market. Remarkably, with the recently opened Ibn Battuta Mall and Mall of the Emirates, and with the forthcoming Dubai Mall, the city's tally of such centres will soon be approaching the thirty mark.

It is also important to note the extent to which Dubai's industrialisation and commercial strategies have also involved a serious commitment to attracting foreign direct investment. In particular, Dubai has constructed a number of 'export processing zones', in which foreign companies can set up camp in a ready-made environment (complete with offices, Internet connections, and in some cases even secretarial staff) that is, of course, free of tax. At the forefront of such developments has been the Jebel Ali Free Zone, southwest of Dubai. Although the original 1975 decision to create Jebel Ali envisaged the zone as simply being Dubai's second port,[14] in 1985 the Dubai Department of Industry began to operate it with the objective of supplying foreign clients with all the necessary administration, engineering and utility services.[15] The zone has expanded from around 300 companies in 1990 to over 2,000 companies today (30 percent of which are European, and 14 percent of which are North American) and has attracted about $4 billion in investments.[16] For high-tech and media companies, other more specialist zones also now exist, including Dubai Internet City and Dubai Media City. Having opened in 2000, their aims were to provide Internet and media-free zones with the entire necessary communications infrastructure in place for prospective computer-oriented firms.[17]

Foreign investment has also been channelled into Dubai's rapidly growing invisibles sector, as the emirate has rapidly expanded its international banking and insurance zones. As late as the 1960s, only two foreign banking houses operated in Dubai (Eastern Bank and the British Bank of the Middle East),[18] whereas today, fuelled by enormous demand and highly conducive conditions, Dubai is now home to dozens of Western and Asian banks including Paribas, Citibank, HSBC, Barclays and Lloyds. Moreover, in 2000 Dubai was the first of the emirates to provide an integrated financial market, and more recently it has opened up the Dubai International Financial Centre.

Attracting foreign investment from individuals has of course been Dubai's much publicised real-estate sector. Since the late 1990s, Dubai has been deliberately circumventing a longstanding federal law which bans property ownership for non-nationals, and, with the backing of the ruler, Sheikh Mohammed bin Rashid Al Maktoum, a number of the city's major developers have launched large-scale multiphase residential projects aimed specifically at either a Western or expatriate Arab clientele. Tellingly, almost all of the adverts for these projects (which are plastered all over the emirate) feature either Western or distinctly non-Emirati nuclear families frolicking on beaches or in gardens in front of their new homes. Significantly, the nature of real-estate promotion in Abu Dhabi is different and more cautious than in Dubai. Adverts feature relatively conservatively dressed Gulf and expatriate Arabs with only the occasional sprinkling of Westerners.

With a new emirate-level law in place in Dubai (allowing foreigners to hold residency visas based on property ownership rather than employment), and with a new federal law having been introduced in late 2005, the sector has enjoyed enormous confidence, boosted by the attraction of large premiums for property speculators, and by the prospects of tax-free rent income for longer-term investors. While the number of these projects has now reached the stage where no one person can keep track, it is nevertheless useful to draw attention to some of Dubai's most ambitious schemes, if only to give an idea of the sheer scale of the strategy and the extent of Dubai's commitment.

The pioneer real-estate developer, Emaar Properties, chaired by the ruler's close ally, Muhammad al-Abbar, launched 'Emirates Hills' in 1997: a golfing-cum-residential project which was the first in the UAE to allow for foreign ownership. Emaar has since been the driving force behind the excavation and development of the Dubai Marina and, more recently, the 'Old Town' and the Burj Dubai project; with over 190 storeys and a dynamic design capable of adjusting to international competition, Emaar insists that the Burj Dubai will be the world's tallest building upon its completion in 2008. Similarly spectacular have been the projects of Nakheel, the developer of the three Palm Island Projects and 'The World': a series of manmade islands and archipelagos for high-end foreign investors. Alongside the Great Wall of China, these are the only manmade constructions visible from space.

Providing downtown, business-centric residences, Dubai Holdings has now launched the 'Business Bay' project: a gigantic artificial canal connecting the creek to a multitude of emerging skyscrapers complete with Venetian-style waterways just behind Sheikh Zayed Road and close to the aforementioned Dubai International Financial Centre. Crucially, almost all properties in these developments are snapped up immediately, and demand is currently outstripping supply. Moreover, although there are undoubtedly long-term risks associated with what many believe to be an overextension of the sector, given that most of the real-estate funds are paid up front by investors (often before the buildings have even emerged from the sand), Dubai is presently in a win-win situation.[19]

As a side note, and although more a legacy of Dubai's *laissez-faire* past than a conscious part of Dubai's current development strategy, it is worth mentioning how this greater flexibility in permitting private ownership of real estate must be regarded as another key factor behind the growth of the commercial sector and the proliferation of shopping malls. Unlike Abu Dhabi, where until very recently most of the land was under government ownership, in Dubai it has been much easier for one individual or a group of investors to buy up many adjacent plots of land, thereby securing enough space for 'megaprojects'. In Abu Dhabi (home to just two major shopping malls) such megaprojects are only really a possibility for powerful businessmen who are either part of, or closely linked to, the ruling family, the best example being Sheikh Suroor bin Muhammed Al Nahayan – the proprietor of the Abu Dhabi Mall and Trade Centre.

Alongside real estate, also attracting foreign currency and boosting the diversification process has been Dubai's rapidly expanding tourism industry, supported by an increasing number of cultural and sporting events. The emirate is now home to over 300 hotels and draws more than 3 million visitors per annum (compared with just 40 hotels and 0.4 million visitors in 1985),[20] many of them flown in courtesy of 'Emirates', Dubai's semi-government-owned and award-winning airline.[21] Moreover, given the major hotel developments that have taken place since 2000, including the Dubai Fairmont, the Dusit Dubai and the Grand Hyatt, and given the only temporary decline in tourism following the September 2001 terrorist attacks in the United States, these positive trends seem set to continue.[22]

The upshot of all of these diversification and foreign investment strategies is that Dubai is now undoubtedly less reliant on its dwindling oil reserves, and is clearly the most integrated into the international system of all of the Gulf states. Indeed, in recent years Dubai has been attracting around 54 percent of all non-oil-related foreign direct investment in the UAE's manufacturing sector. This compares very favourably with Sharjah's share of 21 percent and 'Ajman's share of 10 percent. Significantly, accounting for just 9 percent, Abu Dhabi ranks only fourth, indicating the emirate's described preference for heavier, state-sponsored industries and its markedly different outlook on foreign direct investment.[23] By the mid-1990s Dubai's non-oil sectors were already contributing 82 percent of the emirate's GDP, but most remarkably (as the real estate and tourism strategies began to kick in) since then the non-oil share of GDP has increased to over 94 percent. Moreover, while Dubai's GDP accounts for around 25 percent of the UAE's total, its share of the UAE's total non-oil GDP stands at about 35 percent.[24]

The Ruling Bargain and National Identity

With regard to political stability and security, however, Dubai's eagerness to integrate itself into the international system is likely to have serious consequences in the very near future, and unless properly managed and contained, these may well outweigh the raw economic benefits of its development strategies. As other studies have demonstrated,[25] many of the world's surviving traditional monarchies (most of which are Gulf states) rely upon an extremely delicate balance of legitimacy resources which together make up something of a 'ruling bargain' with the national population. The United Arab Emirates is definitely no exception, as its very survival has rested upon a combination of cultural and religious resources, combined with massive distributions of oil-rent-derived wealth to its citizens, who bask in a carefully constructed national identity. Dubai's diversification does not, of course, upset the wealth distribution component, given that it is still the nationals who own the plots of land that the residential properties, hotels and foreign business parks are built upon. Indeed, although there are a few hidden taxes creeping up on Dubai's nationals (including higher parking fees, uncompetitive monopoly-control-led telecoms prices, and a 10 percent tax on utility payments), and although they may no longer be receiving such blatant oil-financed handouts from the government (as is still the case in Abu Dhabi where nationals receive much larger 'marriage funds', and can expect very generous allowances and free residences), it is important to understand that the vast majority of Dubai nationals are still elevated above the wealth creation process and can still enjoy a rent-based income, albeit a different form of rent.

Dubai's Economic Development and Its Implications for the Ruling Bargain

What Dubai's diversification does upset are the cultural, religious and national identity resources of the bargain. With accelerating foreign ownership, many of the nationals, both young and old, feel that Dubai's development is not really for their benefit any more. As foreigners are beginning to make vast profits out of real estate and other activities that were formerly the preserve of the indigenous population, the monarchy and its cronies are beginning to appear as very obvious clients or intermediaries in a metropole–satellite–chain of dependent relations. In other words, although the money still flows, Dubai nationals realise that their previous membership of a distinct patrimonial elite is now under threat. There are now parts of the city where Dubai nationals feel unwelcome, and to many it feels as if they are living in 'national' ghettos. National dress does not guarantee preferential service, and those nationals who are not *rentiers* are struggling with rising prices, with many now turning to menial employment. Moreover, with the younger generation of nationals now obliged to become fluent in English, the usefulness and status of Arabic, another key component of national identity, has declined.

Not only are formerly exclusive privileges being eroded, but so too is their way of life, as the government continues to bend rules to accommodate the increasing number of non-Arab and non-Muslim foreigners. Most obviously, following an emirate-level decree, the volume of loudspeakers on mosques has been reduced in many residential areas (including those with mixed national and foreign communities such as Umm Suqeim and Jumierah), and previous restrictions on food and drink normally observed during the month of Ramadan are now rarely monitored. Indeed, in many of Dubai's hotels it is perfectly possible to consume alcohol during this month and all other Islamic holidays. Remarkably, during the official mourning period following the death of the ruler of Abu Dhabi, Sheikh Zayed bin Sultan Al Nahayan in November 2004, Dubai chose not to adhere to the UAE-wide prohibition of live music and alcohol lest its tourist industry be affected. Similarly shocking to the local population has been an increase in prostitution. Also worthy of note is the tolerance of homosexuality (which is officially illegal in the UAE and often leads to imprisonment and corporal punishment in Abu Dhabi, Sharjah and the other emirates).

Perhaps most controversial of all has been Dubai's increasing communication with Israel. With its rising profile in the international system, Dubai chose to host the 2003 annual meetings of the World Bank and the IMF and, given that Israel is also a member of these organisations, a delegation had to be invited. When one considers that for more than thirty years all of the GCC states have upheld a total boycott on all Israeli relations and trade, and when one considers that one of the UAE's primary foreign policy objectives (and ideological legitimacy resources) is its support for Palestine against its illegal occupation, one can begin to imagine how dangerous Dubai's strategy has become.

Notes

1. Christopher M. Davidson, 'The Emirates of Abu Dhabi and Dubai: Contrasting Roles in the International System', *Asian Affairs*, vol. XXXVIII, no. 1, 2007, pp. 34–6.

2. Christopher M. Davidson, 'After Sheikh Zayed: The Politics of Succession in Abu Dhabi and the United Arab Emirates', *Middle East Policy*, vol. XIII, no. 1, 2006, pp. 43–5.

3. The Samsung-ADIA complex, despite suffering a major fire in 2004, was completed in 2007, easily eclipsing the Hilton's Burj Baynunah to become Abu Dhabi's tallest building.

4. Personal interviews, Abu Dhabi, June 2005.

5. Oxford Business Group, *Emerging Emirates*, London 2001, p. 43.

6. Personal interviews, Abu Dhabi, June 2005.

7. Oxford Business Group, pp. 90–1.

8. 'Abu Dhabi Shipbuilding Profits Rise', *Gulf News*, 2 August 2005.

9. Al-Sharan International Consultancy, *United Arab Emirates Country Report*, Dubai 2001, pp. 14–5.

10. Dubai's aluminium capabilities fall under the auspices of DUBAL – a semi-government parastatal.

11. Oxford Business Group, pp. 90–1.

12. Christopher M. Davidson, *The United Arab Emirates: A Study in Survival*, Boulder 2005, p. 125.

13. Dubai Department of Ports and Customs, 'Dubai: non-oil foreign trade', in Dubai Department of Economic Development, *Development Statistics*, Dubai 2002, p. 109.

14. Personal interviews with Frauke Heard-Bey, Abu Dhabi, January 2004.

15. Dubai Department of Industry, 'Jebel Ali Free Zone', *Dubai Department of Economic Development Statistics*, Dubai, 2003, p. 241.

16. Dubai Department of Industry, p. 255.

17. Economist Intelligence Unit, *United Arab Emirates*, London 2001, p. 5.

18. Kevin Fenelon, *The United Arab Emirates: An Economic and Social Survey*, London 1973, pp. 80–3.

19. For a more detailed, albeit now slightly dated, discussion, see Davidson, *The United Arab Emirates*, pp. 229–32.

20. Dubai Department of Tourism and Commerce Marketing, 'Hotels and Tourists', in *Dubai Department of Economic Development Statistics*, Dubai, 2003, pp. 167, 172.

21. Davidson, *The United Arab Emirates*, p. 167.

22. Davidson, *The United Arab Emirates*, p. 134.

23. Personal interviews with members of the UAE Ministry of Finance and Industry, Abu Dhabi, January 2004.

24. Personal interviews with members of the UAE Ministry of Planning, Abu Dhabi, January 2004.

25. Davidson, *The United Arab Emirates*, pp. 65–118.

NINE

Debates on Political Reform in the Gulf: The Dynamics of Liberalising Public Spaces

Amr Hamzawy

With the exception of semi-democratic Kuwait, domestic politics in the countries of the Gulf Cooperation Council (GCC) may seem very different from domestic politics in the Arab Near East and North Africa. While the last few years in Morocco, Algeria, Egypt and Lebanon have brought heightened conflicts between regimes and oppositions, electoral surprises and sporadic mass protests, the Gulf has in general remained a place of tranquillity, where stable ruling establishments govern contented populations. Politics in Saudi Arabia, Oman, the United Arab Emirates (UAE), Qatar and Bahrain has been neither marred by struggles over power nor exposed to episodes of ideological polarisation and street mobilisation. In accounting for this 'Gulf uniqueness', analysts have tended to cite a long list of pacifying factors including high standards of living, the absence of pressing socioeconomic crises, the traditional tribal structure of society and the benevolent authoritarianism of Gulf monarchies. Yet political realities on the ground have been far more complex, and thus more interesting, than that.

Since the end of the 1990s, the GCC countries have experienced significant openings in their public spaces. Politics, religion, culture and society have been debated in an unprecedented pluralist manner in domestic television broadcasts and newspapers, on university campuses, on the Internet, and sometimes in government-controlled legislative councils. Previous red lines on official corruption, government accountability and human rights have either lost their significance or are challenged on a daily basis. Rulers have publicly committed to political reforms, and their record on enacting changes will be scrutinised in the public arenas and by the opposition they have come to tolerate – unless they clamp down again on society. The concentration of power has not really altered in the GCC states, with the noteworthy exception of Kuwait. However, the nonviolent opposition has been allowed to criticise government policy publicly and to propose sometimes competing political visions. Both branches of that opposition – the moderate Islamists and the liberals – have been empowered by their integration into the public space, and the ongoing reform debates have inevitably influenced decision-makers, probably more than is obvious at this moment in time.

Socioeconomic transformation at home, post-9/11 pressure and democracy promotion by the West, and globalisation-at-large have driven the political opening in the GCC countries, as elsewhere in the Arab world. In response to these forces for change, most of the Gulf governments have eased their control over and censorship of media outlets. While Oman and Bahrain have legalised private radio stations, the governments of the UAE and Qatar have granted domestic television channels – for example, Dubai TV, Abu Dhabi TV and Qatar TV – greater freedom in debating political events. Liberal venues have emerged and gained momentum – both formal ones such as the National Dialogue Meetings in Saudi Arabia, and informal intellectual forums such as journalists' and university professors' clubs in Bahrain. Improved educational standards have given rise to a Gulf intelligentsia whose members have gradually replaced Near East intellectuals in top positions in the media. Their ascendancy has pushed domestic concerns to the fore, at the expense of all-Arab matters such as the conflict with Israel and relations with the West, and indirectly impelled governments to tolerate increasingly controversial debates on imminent political and social matters. Finally, the relatively free movement of capital and people within the GCC and the similar challenges facing GCC states have allowed the creation of a pan-Gulf public space. The trading of ideas and debates across national borders has evolved into a unique feature of the region. In the absence of a defining ideology or a political grand narrative, pluralism and openness have become structuring norms, calling on GCC governments, media corporations and intellectuals alike to act accordingly.

Political opening in the Gulf has its deficits. With the exception of Kuwait, broad segments of the population have either been left out of the reform debates or shown little interest in debating anything. Religious and tribal authorities have not relinquished their control over informal public spaces, thus undercutting the emergence of a modern public space and limiting its outreach. Where they are permitted to operate, public spaces in the Gulf have been open only to intellectual elites and organised political/social actors. Nor have substantial differences between the GCC countries vanished. It is difficult to put Saudi Arabia, where the royal family has in general ensured the conformity of private media corporations through direct ownership and seldom hesitated to repress or sideline critical voices, in the same category as Bahrain, which has enjoyed liberal press laws since the end of the 1990s.

In spite of all those shortcomings, the trend in the Gulf has been a relative expansion of freedom and a growing degree of pluralism. It has been in this climate that debates on the prospects of political reform in the Gulf have evolved, attracting the attention of policymakers and opinion leaders as well as intellectuals. Additionally, since the terror attacks of 11 September 2001, by hijackers mainly hailing from Saudi Arabia, the GCC states, like other Arab states in the Near East and North Africa, have faced mounting international scrutiny and sporadic American-led diplomatic pressure regarding the status of freedom and human rights in their countries. As the Saudi security services arrested in March 2004 a dozen human-rights activists and intellectuals for calling for more democracy in the kingdom, the incident – by no means an uncommon practice in Saudi Arabia prior to 2001 – received for the first time detailed coverage in the Western press.[1] Various international human-rights organisations condemned the arrests. Most recently, the detention of Hassan Mushaima'a and Abdul-Hadi al-Khawaja – two prominent Shi'i politicians from Bahrain – by local police authorities on 2 February 2007 unleashed only a few hours later a wave of domestic protests and international non-governmental condemnations. The Bahraini government responded by releasing them on the same day.

While governments have responded with promises of gradual measures to open up societies politically, Gulf intellectuals and activists from both the liberal and the moderate-Islamist camps have used the official rhetoric to press their governments to commit and deliver.

Three Actors and the Rules of Debate

Since the oil boom in 1973, citizens of the GCC countries have witnessed a rapid improvement in their standard of living. Per capita income varies across the GCC states but remains remarkably higher than in the rest of the Arab world.[2] Conflicts between the haves and have-nots, which have become a dominant feature of Arab societies of the Near East and North Africa, have been rather muted in the Gulf. Leaving Kuwait aside, the state–society relationship in the Gulf monarchies has been characterised by a specific brand of authoritarianism, driven by the tribal–patriarchal social fabric and less repressive than its counterparts elsewhere in the Arab world. Except for Bahrain, where a Sunni minority rules over a marginalised Shi'i majority, the GCC countries are divided along confessional lines into Sunni majorities, to which the ruling establishments belong, and Shi'i minorities that have hardly any organised political representation.[3] Political parties are banned in the Gulf. Political societies have been allowed to operate and participate in electoral politics – with varying degrees of restrictions – in Kuwait and Bahrain since 2001. In other GCC countries, the opposition lacks any legal status in the political space, but does exist informally or operates as a civil society organisation.

Similar to elsewhere in the Arab world, three major actors have shaped contemporary debates about political reform in the GCC countries: ruling establishments, nonviolent Islamist movements, and liberal organisations. In spite of differences in their local profiles, each of the three has demonstrated across the Gulf – with the exception of Kuwait – considerable harmony when it comes to reform rhetoric and preferences, justifying the collective treatment here of each of the groups.

Traditionally, the Gulf royal families have exercised absolute power over society and the economy. They have resorted to different strategies to generate legitimacy among their populations. Religion, sometimes a specific doctrine such as Wahhabi Islam in Saudi Arabia, and to a lesser extent in Qatar, and traditional values have been employed to secure popular acquiescence. Yet, more significant has been the clever societal balancing implemented by the royal families amid a constant expansion of welfare structures in the GCC countries to offset any potential discontent.

Islamist opposition currents have been on the rise in the Gulf since the late 1970s. Nonviolent Islamists such as the Shi'i-based Wefaq Society in Bahrain have developed a strategic commitment to democratic reform through peaceful social and political participation. Others, like Sunni moderate Islamists in Saudi Arabia, have gone through phases of militant activism, but moved in recent times to favour pushing for gradual openings in their societies. Moderate Islamists have demonstrated their popularity and thus political significance in recent elections across the Gulf. They swept Saudi municipal elections that were held in 2005. The Wefaq Society emerged as the strongest opposition bloc in the Bahraini parliament – Bahrain has a bicameral legislative system with an appointed council and an elected parliament – after the elections of 2006. In contrast, Islamist extremists have lost to a great extent the popular ideological appeal they used to have in the 1980s and 1990s. The intertwined objectives of extremists in the Gulf, establishing an Islamic caliphate and forcing foreign – primarily American – troops out of the region, are not shared by considerable segments of the GCC populations. In today's Gulf politics, Islamist extremists have been reduced to marginal groups that may represent a national security threat in a country like Saudi Arabia, but are politically hardly relevant.

Similar to Islamists, liberals have entered the political scene in the Gulf in the 1970s. In contrast to the Islamists' popularity, liberals have never been able to alter their identity as elitist groups whose members are Western-educated and positioned high up on the socioeconomic ladder. Despite some serious attempts at constituency building through providing social services – the most effective strategy of Islamist movements – by organisations such as the Democratic Progressive Forum in Bahrain and the Kuwait Economic Society, the conservative nature of the GCC societies has structurally limited the appeal of the liberal message. Religious rhetoric and symbolism attract, whereas the focus on personal freedoms and the questioning of traditional value systems both surround liberal organisations with a siege of popular doubts about their intentions. Therefore, liberals have remained the weakest component of the Gulf actors' triangle.

Islamist and liberal activists have been debating the prospects of reform in the Gulf for years, in their mutually antagonistic ways, but the public focused on the debate only after the sweeping move by GCC ruling establishments to appropriate the reform rhetoric and use it for their own purposes in response to international democracy promotion efforts and to domestic demands in some countries such as Saudi Arabia and Bahrain. Starting in 2002, Gulf rulers publicly committed themselves to the implementation of various measures aimed at slightly opening up their polities. While the Saudi government promised to increase the authorities of the Shura Council, the country's consultative body at the national level, and to hold partial municipal elections, in 2003 Qatar changed its constitution to allow citizens to choose thirty out of forty-five members of the Shura Council in competitive elections. In Oman, the government announced a national plan to improve citizens' participation gradually, culminating in holding elections to the Shura Council in 2003. Bahrain legalised political societies in 2001 and allowed for a greater freedom of expression in the public space. Even the UAE rulers, among those most reluctant to embark on the road of political reform, vowed to legalise nongovernmental organisations and to hold partial parliamentary elections.

Although most of these measures have been designed to introduce minor changes at the edges of the political space without challenging the underlying power structures of Gulf authoritarianism – Shura Councils in the GCC countries do not have any real legislative or oversight powers – their implementation unleashed a three-way contest over the reform agenda between ruling establishments, Islamists and liberal activists, one of the unintended consequences of which has been the *de facto* acceptance by Gulf rulers of the plurality of voices and views articulated in the public space.

The sheer asymmetry of power has secured a gatekeeper role for ruling establishments in ongoing reform debates, but Islamists and liberals have considerable influence over both substance and tone. In other words – and once again similar to the situation in much of the remainder of the Arab world – the rulers' reform agenda has not yet become a hegemonic narrative that relegates divergent accounts to the sidelines. Islamists and liberals have kept the strategic advantage gained by being the first to inject concerns about human rights and political freedoms and in choosing the language used to describe their backward condition in the Gulf. The limitations of the official rhetoric, which has failed to address many political and societal deficits sufficiently, also leave vast room for critical insights from the opposition camps.

Although the competition over political reform among the ruling establishments, Islamists and liberals has picked up over the few last years, the Gulf has remained a rather amicable place. Reform debates there are less antagonistic in form and substance than those in other

Arab countries such as Morocco, Egypt, Lebanon and Jordan. There are two possible explanations. On the one hand, except for Kuwait, remarkable political stability has reigned in the Gulf. Changes, even in confessionally heterogeneous Bahrain, have never been anything but gradual, if not downright slow. Therefore the stakes at any given moment, whether for ruling establishments or Islamist or liberal oppositions, are rarely high enough to push them into reductionist 'us versus them' thinking and thus into substantial confrontations. On the other hand, with occasional exceptions such as the ongoing controversy in Saudi Arabia over women's personal freedoms, differences in the three actors' reform platforms have been confined to political issues. The debaters have avoided social and cultural questions such as gender equality and the role of religion in the public space that time and again have deeply divided Gulf societies, splitting them into antagonistic conservative majorities and progressive minorities.

Arguments for Reform

Notwithstanding specific local concerns and temporary debates in each of the GCC countries, two issues have structured the Gulf reform 'talk': the necessity of political reform, and the intertwined ideas of Gulf particularity and reform gradualism (or a go-slow approach). The different positions that ruling establishments, moderate Islamists, and liberal organisations take on those issues strongly influence the decision-making environment in the Gulf. While they have inspired some governments to put reform policies into practice, they have placed others on the defensive. The distribution of political power may not have changed in any meaningful way, yet the pluralist dynamics of debating reform have shaped the preferences of rulers and given both opposition camps a better place at the table.

The starting point for the platforms of all three actors has been the forceful recognition of the need to reform the state–society relationship across the Gulf. While all three have couched their ideas about reform in the language of democracy and good governance, the arguments they put forward to make the case for reform have varied considerably.

Ruling establishments have systematically portrayed political reform as the inevitable product of rapid transformations in the GCC societies; social and economic modernisation, they say, ultimately lead to political modernisation. Thus they have focused on introducing in the state bureaucracy and public institutions administrative reforms designed to bring them up to date with the challenges of economic globalisation, in which the Gulf – because of its oil and gas – is a major player. In other words, grounding the necessity of reform in a reactive logic driven by socioeconomic forces has enabled rulers to leave out the core political issues, including power distribution, popular participation, elections, rulers' accountability and human rights.

Ruling establishments have also advanced a second argument that ties the need for reform to Western initiatives to promote democracy in the Gulf. The official rationale here has depicted the role of the West either as potentially positive and therefore worthy of constructive engagement, or as utterly destructive if left without guidance from Gulf rulers. The governments of Bahrain, Qatar and Oman have responded in a friendly manner to Western efforts at democracy promotion, actively participating in regional and international forums on reform and endorsing various declarations committing themselves to a gradual opening up of their politics. Saudi Arabia and the UAE, on the other hand, have regularly warned the West against interference in the Gulf's domestic affairs and pledged, almost belligerently, to implement reform programmes sensitive to the realities in their countries. Despite the strategic alliance with the West, both Saudi and Emirati ruling establishments have seen in the imposition of Western reform benchmarks an imminent threat to their stability, and thus rejected them. In March 2004, a few months after the Bush Administration announced its Broader Middle East and North Africa Initiative for reform, the Saudi foreign minister Prince Sa'ud al-Faysal was quoted as saying that 'his government is not waiting for direction from outside' and that 'reforms will be introduced in keeping with the wishes of the society.'⁴ Similar statements were made by Emirati officials.

Notwithstanding the differences between the two arguments, both have made it easier for Gulf ruling establishments to legitimise cosmetic or limited changes, passing them off as signs of significant reform policies. Qatar and Oman, for example, have devoted much of their reform energy to appointing women to public office and have succeeded, in spite of the absence of any democratic substance in their countries' politics, in framing the appointment of female ministers as a great achievement of enlightened rulers friendly to the West, forging ahead to democratise their conservative societies. In contrast, Gulf ruling establishments critical of the West have cast themselves as the true defenders of Gulf authenticity in the face of Western assaults. The official line has elevated changes as limited as the Saudi municipal elections of 2005 or the UAE legislative elections in late 2006 – in which the Emirati electorate was reduced to a government-appointed electoral board – to the status of strategic milestones on a reform path that steers clear of corrupting Western influences.

To sum up, acknowledgment of the compelling necessity of reform in the Gulf has been reduced in rulers' reform agendas to justifications for either state-led administrative modernisation or limited political reforms introduced and managed from the top with no significant impacts on power distribution in the GCC countries.

To offset the official rhetoric and put what they see as core political issues to the fore in public debates, both Islamist and liberal oppositions work from a rather negative reading of contemporary Gulf realities. Critical of rulers' depiction of socioeconomic modernisation as a linear success story, Islamists and liberals alike highlight persistent and worsening deficiencies in the GCC countries, such as the widening gap between rich and poor and rising levels of governmental corruption. In both camps, reform measures are seen as the only viable strategy for overcoming those deficiencies.

In order to avoid falling into the rulers' administrative-modernisation trap and reducing inequality and corruption to mere technical

shortcomings that could be corrected once efficient modern bure-
aucracies have been installed, the opposition has deepened the
debate to include issues at the centre of the desired democratic state–
society relationship. With varying degrees of rhetorical harshness,
Islamists and liberals have attributed inequality and corruption to the
concentration of power and absence of an established rule of law in the
Gulf. The reform measures they suggest focus on limiting the power of
ruling establishments through institutionalised checks and balances
among the branches of government; holding rulers accountable for
their policies; introducing elements of popular participation into the
national decision-making process through competitive legislative and
municipal elections; and vesting some oversight powers in the Shura
Councils to move beyond the current status of advisory bodies.

Although Islamists and liberals have turned around the official
rhetoric to arrive at the same political reforms, they advance different
arguments in making their case in the public space. Islamists have
made use of the well-entrenched religious rhetoric about equality,
justice and *shura* (the Islamic principle of popular consultation) to
remind Gulf citizens of the 'true' Islamic governance values and of
how terribly far their modern societies have drifted from them. In the
Islamists' universe, democratic reforms aim to recapture an ideal past
in which faithful rulers of Muslim communities ensured equality and
protected citizens' rights. Liberal activists, for their part, have walked
a fine line between presenting democratic reform as a universal norm
that can no longer be violated and presenting it as the only reform that
satisfies the aspirations of the young majorities in the GCC countries.
Faced with ruling establishments' vigorous approval or condemnation
of Western democracy promotion, and Islamists' appeal to religious
values, Gulf liberals have used two rhetorical strategies to garner public
support for their vision. They invoke a normative plea for a democratic state–society relationship and cast democracy as the inevitable
outcome of a pressing demographic factor, the young average age –
mid-twenties – of the populations of the Gulf societies.

The second feature structuring the debates in GCC countries on political reform has been the unequivocal consensus among ruling establishments and Islamist oppositions on so-called Gulf particularity and reform gradualism. Both rulers and Islamists cite history, religion and culture to assert the interrelated needs for a specific Gulf path to reform and a slow pace while on it. Yet in terms of the policy shifts the two sides advocate, the outcome has been rather contradictory.

Justifying their marginal, if not merely cosmetic, reform measures, GCC ruling establishments have tended to put the blame for the lack of democratic mechanisms and the weakness in governance standards on their countries' societies, saying that they are by nature inhospitable to reform. According to this narrative, the region is traditional, religious, conservative, and thus ill prepared for democracy. Royal families in Saudi Arabia and the UAE have explained their unwillingness to establish real parliaments and hold free elections on the grounds that their people are averse to such 'conflict-inducing' affairs. In both countries, bans on political parties and associations have been officially attributed to a social fabric that purportedly favours tribal affiliations and direct consultation with the rulers over modern interest representation.[5] In other countries, such as Qatar and Oman, the rulers craft an image that is centred on their enlightened resolve to gradually persuade unwilling populations of the merits of modern reforms. There are still significant differences between Gulf royal families on reform, but all agree on a working formula of measured changes to ensure that reform does not get out of hand.

In the final analysis, the official rhetoric on particularity and gradualism has narrowed the scope of potential reforms by excluding measures central to democratic transformation, such as free elections and freedom of assembly, because they might jeopardise the authority of ruling establishments. Gulf rulers have sought to use debates on reform to inject authoritarian elements into the public space and to take the wind out of any demands for a significant opening of the political space to competition and, eventually, to the prospect of the alternation of power.

In contrast, Islamist oppositions have fashioned an extensive rhetoric around the issues of particularity and gradualism to make certain that any future reform will not alter the current centrality of religion in the GCC countries. In other words, Islamists paint a picture of the Gulf similar to that of the ruling establishments, but use the religious and conservative preferences attributed to the Gulf's people to mark those areas in the social fabric that should not be touched by political reforms. Distinct from rulers' fear that political reforms might undercut their authority, the Islamist opposition is obsessed by the possibility of losing its monopoly over questions of morality and good–evil dualities in the public space in the event of an unrestrained implementation of liberal reforms – which, in Islamists' minds, are always Western-inspired. For example, while Islamists have come out strongly across the Gulf in favour of opening up the political space to allow for a degree of competition and of holding free elections, they have been rather reluctant in every GCC country except Bahrain to endorse women's right to participate in elections as voters and candidates. Islamist activists and intellectuals have aggressively defended this illiberal stance by stressing the need to protect true Islamic teachings – as they understand them – from reform measures that threaten to violate their essence.[6]

Faced with an official rhetoric on particularity and gradualism designed to preserve the political order amid managed reforms from the top and an Islamist argument intent on protecting the place of religion in the public order, liberal opposition groups in the Gulf have had almost no choice but to defy the status quo consensus. While acknowledging the organisational difficulties that face them in GCC countries, liberal voices have maintained that implementing significant reforms that open up the political space to true competition would prepare the Gulf for a democratic transition. Lacking regional success stories, liberals allude to cases of successful democratisation outside the Arab world (primarily in South America and Eastern Europe). Liberal oppositions have also sought to appropriate in reverse the two concepts of particularity and gradualism, defining them in a reform-friendly manner.

Accordingly, liberal rhetoric acknowledges that Gulf particularity and a desire for gradualism basically rule out the possibility of big, sudden leaps towards a democratic political order in the GCC countries. Liberal activists, however, have dismissed rulers' notions of measured reforms as an authoritarian delaying tactic and have called for clear timelines for the gradual introduction of free elections and other policies conducive to real democratic openings. Here again, as in the debate over the necessity of reform, liberals have cited the democratic aspirations of young Gulf majorities to legitimate their demands. Furthermore, they have contested the Islamist take on particularity, accusing Islamists of claiming a monopoly over religion to advance their political objectives. To divert attention from the popularity of Islamist movements, the liberal opposition presents a narrative of Gulf societies in which conservative legacies do battle with a rising liberal doctrine that will ultimately prevail.

Yet the liberal challenge to the official and Islamist rhetoric on particularity and gradualism has not generated much support among the people of the GCC states. Running counter to the liberal vision of young majorities with democratic aspirations, fears of unintended consequences of political reform seem to win out over the dream of democratic transformation. Indeed, the majority of people in the region have always seemed fairly content with the way things are and thus obliged to contemplate the potential effect of any reforms on their traditional way of life and of course on the high standard of living that oil money has given them. After all, the conservative saga about the GCC countries has never lacked for confirming evidence. Only in the few cases in which the Islamist opposition's rejection of reform has gone too far for rulers' taste – such as in the Bahraini controversy over female candidates in parliamentary elections – has the liberal criticism of the status quo taken on new importance. In order to garner popular acceptance for women's candidacy in the 2006 parliamentary elections, the ruling establishment – through the governmental Supreme Council for Women – supported female candidates and used liberal arguments to counterbalance the *de facto* rejectionist attitude of both Shi'i and Sunni Islamist movements, which put only men on their electoral lists.

Missing Elements – Citizenship and Public Property

Apart from the controversies over reform of the state–society relationship and particularity and gradualism in the GCC countries, public debate in the Gulf has touched the fringes of substantial political issues, such as citizenship and public property rights.

In spite of the significant confessional divisions in the GCC countries between the Sunni and Shi'i communities, Gulf ruling establishments as well as Islamist and liberal oppositions have generally chosen not to tackle the issue of citizenship rights and equality between the confessions. Sectarian tensions on the regional scene and the imbalance in the Gulf population structure make open debate on those issues even less likely.

Instead of becoming a role model for democratic transition, post-Saddam Iraq has degenerated into a horrifying case of state failure and spiralling sectarian violence. Both Gulf rulers and the mostly Sunni-dominated Islamist movements have systematically invoked the 'Iraq factor' to instil in people the fear of sectarian conflict. Their rhetoric has succeeded either in imposing a remarkable silence in the public space with regard to existing inequalities between Sunni and Shi'i citizens, or in portraying marginal correctives introduced by the rulers, especially in Saudi Arabia, as significant steps toward equality for Shi'i communities in the Gulf. The liberal opposition – and for that matter, Shi'i activists – go along with that, fearing popular mistrust or contempt should they include equal citizenship rights in their current reform debates. The imbalance in the population between native-born citizens and foreign inhabitants, mostly guest workers and their families in countries such as the UAE and Qatar, where foreigners represent a clear majority – 80 percent in both according to figures compiled by Human Rights Watch – also makes all three actors wary of opening up a Pandora's box of conflict over which community is entitled to what rights.

The only Gulf country that has defied this pattern of ignoring the issue of citizenship is Bahrain. Amid a growing political dynamism in the kingdom in recent years, the traditionally underprivileged Shi'i majority has positioned citizenship rights at the forefront of its reform advocacy. Especially the Shi'i Islamist opposition led by the Wefaq Society has relentlessly called on the government of King Hamad bin Isa al-Khalifa to ensure equal political, economic and religious rights for Shi'i and Sunni citizens. To diffuse doubts about their allegiance and sectarian aspirations, Shi'i groups – apart from a few marginal voices – have couched their demands in professions of an undivided loyalty to the nation-state of Bahrain. Although the Sunni ruling establishment refused for a long time to give in to the demands of the Shi'i majority, believing that would ultimately undermine its authority, it has changed course to some extent in recent years and allowed for greater degrees of political participation by Shi'i citizens. As noted earlier, the Wefaq Society became the strongest opposition bloc in the parliament after the elections of 2006.

Besides the *de facto* red line imposed on public debating of citizenship in most GCC countries, talk about public property has been systematically suppressed by the ruling establishments. It is a well-known secret that Gulf royal families have never relinquished their absolute control of strategic state resources – the oil and mineral wealth as well as the vast public lands. Although the GCC rulers have spent some of the proceeds on creating and expanding social welfare structures, it is striking that the expansion of freedom and the growing degree of pluralism in the public space have not led to challenges to this archaic feature of the state–society relationship in the Gulf. Notwithstanding the varying degrees of openness in the GCC political systems, this fact – just like the sidelining of debate on equal citizenship rights – unmistakably demonstrates the real upper limits on the evolving pluralism in the Gulf.

Notes

1. The arrest was reported by the Associated Press and covered by prominent media outlets in the United States and Britain, including CBS and BBC news. Later in April the *Washington Post* ran a story describing the various obstacles facing Saudi reformers which also covered news of the activists who were arrested. See David B. Ottaway 'US-Saudi Relations Show Signs Of Stress: Reformers labeled "Agents of America"', *Washington Post*, 21 April 2004, p. A16.

2. International Monetary Fund, World Economic Outlook Database.

3. The State Department's 2007 *International Regions Freedoms Report* estimates that Shi'is constitute 70 percent of the population in Bahrain, 30 percent in Kuwait, 10 percent in Qatar, 15 percent in the UAE, 10–15 percent in Saudi Arabia and less than 5 percent in Oman.

4. In his address at the European Policy Centre on 19 February 2004 Prince Sa'ud al-Faysal stated that reform 'may be seen as slow or less impressive to some, but if reforms are to endure and be effective, they have to respond to the will of the people and maintain the unity of the nation'.

5. For more on such debates in Saudi Arabia, see 'Can Saudi Arabia reform itself?' *ICE Middle East Report*, no. 38, 14 July 2004 and Amr Hamzawy, 'The Saudia Labyrinth: Evaluating the Current Political Opening', Carnegie Paper no. 68, Carnegie Endowment for International Peace, 2006.

6. A case in point is that of Kuwait. For a long time, Islamist parliamentarians allied themselves with traditionalist forces to block any legislative initiatives to grant women full political rights. It was not until May 2007 that the Kuwaiti parliament yielded to popular and governmental pressures on this matter.

TEN

Gulf Societies: Coexistence of Tradition and Modernity

Lubna Ahmed al-Kazi

The Arab Gulf countries – Bahrain, Kuwait, Qatar, Oman, Saudi Arabia and the United Arab Emirates – differ not only in geographic expanse, but also in population size. While Saudi Arabia is the largest with an area of 850,000 square miles and a population of nearly 30 million, Qatar has an area of 4,000 square miles and a population of less than a million. Whatever their size, these countries share a similar culture and a common history and they are also based on nearly identical political economies.

All monarchies, they acquired immense wealth due to rising oil revenues, mainly in the 1960s and 1970s, embarking then on rapid development. All six countries established welfare states with free education, health and social services. This was not only to redistribute wealth but, as oil is an exhaustible resource, they saw investment in their human capital as the way to sustainable development. Over the past three to four decades, populations have undergone dramatic transformations. With better healthcare, the age distribution has changed. Education has led to the entry of nationals in larger numbers into the workforce. Preoccupation with study and work has led to marrying at later ages, and so on. This chapter will briefly discuss some consequences of changes in education, healthcare, work and politics.

Education

Free education from kindergarten to the highest level is available to all nationals. Girls are encouraged to complete higher education and, as they obtain better grades than their male counterparts, they outnumber them in universities, as Figure 1 reveals. Because girls obtain higher grades in Kuwait, the state university requires lower grades from male students in order to enable men to enrol. Young women are not concentrated in the traditional colleges such as education, humanities and social sciences, but in Kuwait and Saudi Arabia also outnumber males in the colleges of science and medicine. Access to free education has substantially delayed the entry of youth into the labour force.

Figure 1: Gross Enrolment Ratios in Tertiary Education in Gulf Countries, 2001–2002

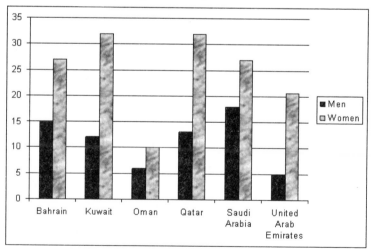

Source: http://www.escwa.org.lb/gsp/statistics/main.html

As for adult literacy rates in 2003, they were over 70 percent for women and over 80 percent for men in the GCC countries. As Table 1 indicates, Oman has the lowest literacy rate and a gender gap of 16 percent (i.e. 16 percent higher literacy among males), whereas in Qatar and the United Arab Emirates women have higher literacy rates than males by 3.5 and 5.5 percent respectively. All Gulf countries have adult literacy programmes and provide incentives for adults to enrol.

Table 1: Literacy rates in GCC countries by sex, 2000–2005

Country		Literacy Rates		Gender Gap
		Men	Women	
1	Bahrain	92	85	7
2	Kuwait	85	82	3
3	Oman	83	67	16
4	Qatar	81.5	85	-3.5
5	Saudi Arabia	85	71	14
6	United Arab Emirates	76	81.5	-5.5

Source: http://www.escwa.org/statistics/edu

Labour Force Participation

With better education, the proportion of nationals in the labour force has risen in all Gulf countries. The increase has been more significant for women, as revealed in Table 2. 'Over the past two decades, between 1980 and 2000, the participation of women in the labour force more than doubled in Bahrain, Kuwait, Qatar and Saudi Arabia, while it almost tripled in Oman and the United Arab Emirates.'[1] In addition to the growing proportion of women in the labour force officially recorded, there is the additional amount of those who work in home-based businesses or have licences in the names of their male family members. These figures are omitted from formal labour statistics.

Table 2: Trend Related to the Proportion of Women
in the Labour Force, 1980–2000

	Country	1980	2000
1	Bahrain	10.9	20.8
2	Kuwait	13.1	31.3
3	Oman	6.2	17.1
4	Qatar	6.7	15.0
5	Saudi Arabia	7.6	16.1
6	United Arab Emirates	5.1	14.8

Source: Adapted from *Women and Men in the Arab Countries: Employment*, ESCWA/
Stat/2002/2,28, Table1, p.3.

The gender gap in economic activity rate – the differential between the activity rate of women and men – is narrowest in Kuwait and widest in Saudi Arabia, at 35 and 65 percent respectively.[2] A possible explanation for this wide discrepancy is that Kuwait is largely urban and offers numerous choices for women to work. In Saudi Arabia, by contrast, the choices for women are more restrictive in rural areas, and women's work outside the home is not viewed favourably. Women cannot practise law in Saudi Arabia but they have joined the medical profession or have become successful business entrepreneurs. Female banking sections and female clinics were traditional solutions to adapting to change within acceptable boundaries. In Kuwait, women have law offices, manage their own businesses and, as engineers, are on construction sites overseeing projects. In the banking sector, female applicants outnumber males for new positions. Figure 2 gives data for gender activity in all GCC countries.

The concentration of nationals in the government sector is a problem in part because it has led to hidden unemployment of nationals. Recent efforts to channel nationals to the private sector have had some positive results. In Kuwait, there has been a rise in new entrants into the private sector, both male and female. One incentive has been a labour support allowance that the government has now given workers in the private sector.

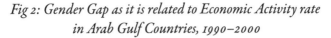

Fig 2: Gender Gap as it is related to Economic Activity rate in Arab Gulf Countries, 1990–2000

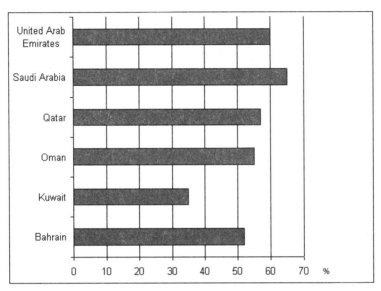

Sources: ESCWA, Compendium of Social Statistics and Indicators, fifth issue, 2001 (E/ ESCWA/2001/10) (Sales No. A/E .02 II.L.5); Bahrain Ministry of Cabinet Affairs, Central Statistical Organisation, Basic Results: Population, Housing, Buildings and Establishment Census, Part One, 2001. Adapted from Women and Men in the Arab Countries: Employment, Chart 1, p. 4

Though women are not paid less for the same job, they are often prevented from moving up the occupation ladder at equal rates. The percentage of women in the higher echelons of decision-making positions is low. Early retirement of women after fifteen or twenty years of service further restricts their upward mobility.

Marriage and Divorce

Two decades ago, women in the Gulf typically married in their teens. With increasing interest in completing education, marriage has been delayed on average to the mid-twenties, except in Oman. Studies have shown that more educated women marry later than their less-educated counterparts.[3] Furthermore, with education, work and mobility, men and women are marrying outside the extended family. First cousin marriage is no longer the norm.

Not only is marriage delayed, but there is also concern with the growing proportion of never-married males. In some Gulf countries such as Kuwait and the United Arab Emirates, governments have tried to encourage youth to marry by giving financial allowances. In Kuwait, a man on his first marriage receives 4,000 Kuwaiti Dinars (equal to approx £8,000), but only if he marries a native. There is also a wife's monthly allowance for life. In the UAE, the government wants to prevent nationals from marrying foreigners, leaving UAE women with little prospect of marriage. The Marriage Fund Foundation, started in the early 1990s, gives loans to low-income nationals if they marry native women. With the birth of each child, 20 percent of the loan is exempted. Saudi Arabia, Qatar and Bahrain also have measures to encourage youth to marry.

As in many modernising societies, divorce rates have steadily increased in the Gulf region. Although there is no data for the same year in all six countries, studies reveal that the lowest divorce rate of 17.7 percent is in Bahrain in 2001 and the highest in Qatar at 36.5 percent in 1997.[4] It was 32.8 percent in Kuwait in 2006.[5] With the gradual disappearance of the extended family in most Gulf countries, although at a slower rate in Saudi Arabia and Oman, some divorcees and widows prefer to live on their own with their children rather than remarry. In Kuwait, the state provides housing and allowances for divorcees who have low incomes.[6]

Health and Population Growth

Another indicator of human development is the availability of health services. In the 1950s and early 1960s, the Gulf countries had very young populations due to high fertility and short life expectancy. With the establishment of hospitals and free clinics, nationals are living longer. Life expectancy ranged from 70.5 years in Qatar to 77 years in Kuwait in 2005.[7] The gender gap is relatively narrow, with women living three to four years longer. With more aged in the population, the governments have increased relevant services. There are mobile free health services for the aged in Kuwait, for example. This facility is meant to discourage putting the old in homes for the aged and to help working family members who cannot take them to the clinics.

Migrant majorities in the GCC countries have caused governments to encourage high fertility among nationals. Kuwait gives a monthly allowance for each child to the Kuwaiti father, who is the head of the household. Nationals can also get a loan to build their homes, so as to encourage larger families. Nevertheless, with increasing education and more career ambitions, young Kuwaitis are having fewer children. Decline in family size is ubiquitous in the Gulf and is positively correlated with the educational level of the married partners.

Political Participation

Political participation has always been a topic of heated debate in the Gulf region. Kuwait is the only country that has had a functioning parliament since the 1960s. Bahrain suspended its parliament in the 1970s for over two decades. Women were excluded from voting and standing in both countries until recently. After three decades of lobbying and petitioning, which began to gain momentum with youth joining the women's movement, the Kuwaiti parliament finally voted to grant women full political rights in May 2005. The first election with female participation was held in Kuwait in July 2006. In Bahrain, women were granted suffrage in 2002. In the November 2006 parliamentary election only one Bahraini woman was successful, having been elected unopposed. In 1999, Qatar had its first elections in which women took part, but none was successful.

The other three GGC countries, Saudi Arabia, Oman and United Arab Emirates, have recently held municipal elections, which indicated a willingness to encourage greater involvement of the people. It is true that only men voted in Saudi Arabia and not even in all regions, but this was a beginning. In the United Arab Emirates, a woman won a seat in the Federal National Council Elections in December 2006, which is a first for Gulf women in an election. These changes are historic, and the involvement of women has led to a better understanding of their needs and a greater awareness among women on how to lobby for their causes. Issues like the Family Law, national women married to non-nationals, and women and decision-making positions are now being discussed by women activists across the Gulf. Previously unheard-of agendas are now in the limelight. Though change has been slow, the perception in the Gulf is that the demands of the people made it happen.

Conclusion

Women and youth are at the centre of change in GCC countries. All GCC nationals share a sense that economic change is having profound social repercussions, including the possible loss of their distinctive identity, which they greatly fear. It was inevitable that educated women would begin formulating ideas of social justice and the issues that had been neglected for decades would gain momentum because 'they are a product of socioeconomic development and change but are themselves spurring development and change'.[8] Previously, complaints that the family was in danger were often voiced. Now, in most instances, it is the father, mother, daughter and son who are working together to lead GCC societies forward. The visibility of women is not seen as a threat to a patriarchal order, but as a sign to show the world that GCC societies are no longer gender biased and are as progressive as others.

Notes

1.   Economic and Social Commission for Western Asia, *Women and Men in the Arab Countries: Employment*, Escwa/Stat/2002/2, 28 March 2002, p. 3.

2.   Economic and Social Commission for Western Asia, *Women and Men in the Arab Countries: Employment*, Escwa/Stat/2002/2, 28 March 2002, p. 4.

3.   Economic and Social Commission for Western Asia, *Women and Men in the Arab Countries: Employment*, Escwa/Stat/2002/2, 28 March 2002, p. 4.

4.   Yahya al-Haddad, *Major Trends Affecting Families: a Background Document*, Report for United Nations, Department of Economic and Social Affairs, Division for Social Policy and Development, Programme on the Family, 2005.

5.   Lubna al-Kazi.

6.   Lubna al-Kazi, 'Divorce a Structural Problem Not Just a Personal Crisis', *Journal of Comparative Family Studies*, University of Calgary, vol. 38.

7.   Gender Statistics Programme in the Arab Countries, http://www.escwa. Org.Lb/Gsp/Statistics/Main.html.

8.   Valentine M. Moghadam, *Modernizing Women: Gender and Social Change in the Middle East*, Boulder, Colorado 2003, p. 278.

Conclusion

Alanoud Alsharekh

The contributors to the conference and the book based on it have managed to capture the essence of the elusive notion of popular culture. This task was all the more difficult because of the setting in GCC countries, which have been subjected to caricature by others and to romantic notions in the minds of many natives themselves. As the world shrinks into an ever-more-uniform global village as a result of such as iPods, Internet downloads and satellite television, all of which contribute to a universal popular culture, many natives of the GCC cling to a manufactured, glorious past to reduce anxieties resulting from living in two cultures. The subjects of external caricatures and internal cultural cross-pressures are dealt with extensively in the preceding chapters.

The latter in particular are of such importance they need to be stressed here. Manufactured cultural inheritance, such as the seafaring lifestyle of yore that all GCC states cling to, has penetrated these societies. It is reflected in exaggerated Bedouin accents in youth who have never ventured into the desert, and in a celebration of nomadic poetry by those who know enough to appreciate it but are unable to repeat or truly understand it. It also manifested itself in attempts by GCC citizens to attempt to mould something that is uniquely theirs within the larger, global framework. This is indicated by their giving the adjectival poetry style of the Peninsula an English twist, or in manufacturing an Arabian version of classical orientalist projection that owes as much to modern technology as to the heritage of the past. Architecture, such as the Burj al-Arab tower in Dubai, art galleries that showcase indigenous talent, and new glossy cultural magazines, such as *Canvas* and *Alef*, which deal with fashion and art, are all amalgams of the old and the new, the innately local and the transnational.

As is typical of academic conferences, some valuable presentations and discussions are not included in the book that follows. A brief mention here of some of these contributions is worthwhile, as it illustrates further aspects of innovative contributions that the GCC states are making to world culture as they imbibe from it and as they seek to counter stereotyped images, such as those of terrorist breeding grounds, or decadent wealth and corruption found in such books as *Oil Sheikhs*.[1] Abdalla Al Thani, for example, spoke of the impact the newly established Ivy League and other universities with local branches are having on education in the area. Saeed al Hajiri of the UAE explained how economic factors are making such changes in education absolutely necessary, since the demands for a competent – indeed competitive – workforce have made the arrival of such institutions that cater to students who cannot afford to travel abroad a necessity. Quality education for an ever larger percentage of young age cohorts is impacting on GCC popular culture, and deeply affects the social structure of these states, as more and more people access what was an exclusive and elitist rite of passage in the past. Ghanim al Najjar and other panellists from Kuwait explained how the established kinship and *diwaniyya* systems governing traditional politics were being undermined by transparency and information accessibility. They discussed how youths, who constitute a majority now in GCC populations, are well acquainted with cyberspace and capable of challenging the pre-existing political order, which was based on information deficits and exclusivity.

Majed al Sabah of Kuwait noted the impact of emerging local tastes on luxury goods markets, manifested by established and entrenched names in the fashion world, such as Prada and Missoni, to design niche items solely for GCC consumers. Typically these products reflect a European twist on traditional Arab women's garb, thereby fusing the old and established local look with what appears on the fashion catwalks in Milan.[2]

The pattern that emerges time and again from examining both the outward manifestations of the popular and the more invisible institutions governing the political cultures of the GCC, is how, in spite of a plethora of options, the people of these states choose the traditional, or a reinterpretation of the traditional, over other, perhaps more consistently 'modern', alternatives. In spite of their flair for cutting-edge fashion, the majority of young people in the GCC choose to live their lives in traditional attire passed on from one generation to another. They also comply with the kinship-system-dictated social and political code inherited from tribal backgrounds, as discussed in greater detail in our previous publication, *The Gulf Family: Kinship Policies and Modernity*.[3] Perhaps this can be understood as a backlash against the 'Other' – the great number of foreigners working and living in GCC states. This pressure is intensified in Dubai, Abu Dhabi, Qatar and elsewhere as they open up to tourists. Threatened by these encounters and having been accused of 'importing culture',[4] as one journalist described the opening of prestigious museums such as the Guggenheim in the UAE, while accused of exporting terrorism and fundamentalist thought, it is no wonder that the people of the Gulf react defensively at times.

Our panellists evaluated the impact of discriminatory regulations when it came to trading, housing, even schooling of foreign citizens in the GCC, and how much that was part of the prevalent popular culture. They also noted how it was being countered by rapidly changing legislation in some GCC states. They further noted that, despite cultural anxiety resulting from these external challenges, the GCC states have a history of rubbing shoulders with different cultures, including in pre-oil times with the people of Iran, India, Africa, Turkey and the Levant. They absorbed elements of these cultures into their own heritage, traditions, even their language. So reinterpreting foreign elements within indigenous practices and beliefs is a long-established tradition in the Gulf. Today, the Gulf is more into Hollywood than Bollywood. The Western military presence and the economic one of malls and fast-food outlets are coupled with tales of moral confusion, best highlighted in the story of the Bahraini princess who ran off with a US serviceman, better known as *The Princess and the Marine*.[5] It remains to be seen what the long-term impact this cultural fusion will have on the area, in both its popular cultural and its political identity.

Notes

1. Linda Blandford, *Oil Sheikhs (Inside the Supercharged World of the Petrodollar)*, London 1977. The inscription on the back cover reads: 'Who are the oil sheikhs? To find out the truth behind this most powerful world force, the author toured the Gulf states, entering the curious closed world of the super rich.' This book gained notorious popularity in the late 1970s at the height of the standoff concerning oil prices between Saudi Arabia and the USA, and perpetuated the image of the oppressive and debauched GCC male and the repressed and sex-starved female that plays into Western stereotypes to this day.

2. In fact, Majed's new project at the revamped Battersea Power Station in London seeks to bring the traditional Arabian souk to Western consumers in 2011.

3. Alanoud Alsharekh ed., *The Gulf Family: Kinship Policies and Modernity*, London 2007.

4. Youssef Ibrahim, 'Can Culture Be Bought in the Gulf?', *The New York Sun*, 5 February 2007.

5. With the influx of hundreds of thousands of US servicemen into the conservative GCC states following the erection of military bases after Operation Desert Storm and the liberation of Kuwait in 1991, there was a widespread fear of the corruption of generations of young girls, and other trends symptomatic of general amorality. The much-hyped love affair and subsequent marriage of a member of the Bahraini ruling family and a US marine stationed in Bahrain in 1999 was the ultimate symbol of this danger, seen in her defiance of traditional gender roles, kinship policies and God in her actions. The princess and her lover, who managed to escape to the US, were much feted by the media, meriting an Oprah Winfrey appearance and even a television movie that was aired in 2001.

Notes on Contributors

Lubna Ahmed al-Kazi is Associate Professor of Sociology at Kuwait University, where her principal areas of interest are labour force and migration, human resource development, gender studies, social problems (such as divorce), population studies and youth and social awareness. She has written widely on development and social and cultural change in Gulf societies and combined her academic work with consultancy work for, among others, the United Nations and the Kuwaiti Ministry of Information, where she was part of a team devising a master plan of tourism in Kuwait.

Dr al-Kazi is also an active member of the Association of Sociologists in Kuwait, the Kuwaiti Women's Cultural and Social Society, the Kuwaiti Women's Network and the International Sociological Association.

Mohammed A. Alkhozai is currently responsible for managing degree programmes and executive development and education programmes with the Bahrain Institute of Banking and Finance (BIBF). Previously, he held the position of Director of Culture and Arts and Director of Publications at the Ministry of Information in Bahrain and has also lectured on English at the Teacher Training College in Bahrain.

Mohammed Alkhozai graduated with a BA in English Literature from the University of Cairo, Egypt. He received his master's degree from the University of Leeds and his doctorate from the School of Oriental and African Studies, specialising in comparative literature and Arabic drama.

Dr Alkhozai is a member of a number of professional and learned societies, including the British Society for Middle Eastern Studies, Middle East Studies Association of North America, Bahrain Management Society, Bahrain Society for Training and Development, and the Bahrain Historical and Archaeological Society. He is a member of the Board of Trustees of the University of Bahrain. He is a past member of the National Council for Culture, Arts and Literature, Past President of the Oruba Club and Past President of the Bahrain Chess Federation.

Dr Alkhozai has published and translated a number of books and written on dramatic and literary criticism.

Alanoud Alsharekh is a member of the Advisory Council of the London Middle East Institute at SOAS. She is a specialist in feminist literature in the Arab Middle East and held teaching posts at both Kuwait University and the Gulf University of Science and Technology before heading the Humanities Department at the Kuwait Branch of the Arab Open University. She serves on the boards of a number of NGOs and philanthropic organisations and has represented the Kuwaiti Government both in an official capacity, and as a civil society group member, to the French Government, the United Nations and the EU Parliament. She has lectured in many local and international institutions, including Uppsala University, Sweden, and has written several articles and two books on women in the Arab world. Dr Alsharekh is one of the few individual recipients of a Middle East Partnership Initiative (MEPI) grant and works as a gender politics consultant for organisations such as UNIFEM, Freedom House and the UNDP on projects in Kuwait and the GCC.

Mohammed al-Mutawa is Associate Professor of Sociology at the United Arab Emirates University where he was previously Vice Dean of the Faculty of Humanities and Social Sciences. He is editor-in-chief of the *Journal of Social Affairs*. His books include T*he Development and Social Change in the UAE, The Consumption Culture* and *New*

Trends and *Social Problems in the UAE* while his articles have appeared in *International Sociology*, *Al Bas'ir*, *Journal of Social Sciences*, *Journal of Gulf Studies* and *Arabian Peninsula*, among others.

Hasan al-Naboodah has been the director of the Zayed Center for Heritage and History in al-'Ain since its foundation in March 1999. He is Professor of History at the United Arab Emirates University, specialising in the early and medieval eras of Islam.

Abdullah Baabood is a businessman and an academic from Oman with over fifteen years of international business experience. His academic interests include the GCC and its economic, political and social development, as well as GCC external relations. He has published and presented at conferences, seminars and workshops on this subject. Dr Baabood is a graduate in Business, Marketing and Economics and he holds an MBA in Business Administration, and an MA and a PhD in International Relations. He is a coordinator of the Cambridge Arab Media Project at the Centre of Middle Eastern and Islamic Studies, University of Cambridge. He also holds several board memberships in a number of organisations in the GCC and the UK as well as being a member of a number of professional and academic institutions.

Christopher Davidson is a Lecturer in Middle Eastern Politics at the Institute for Middle Eastern and Islamic Studies at the University of Durham. He is a former Assistant Professor of Political Science at Zayed University, on both the Abu Dhabi and Dubai campuses, and is the author of the recent book, *The United Arab Emirates: A Study in Survival*. In addition Dr Davidson has published articles relating to the UAE and Kuwait in *Middle East Policy*, *Asian Affairs*, *Middle Eastern Studies* and with the Oxford Business Group. He has provided consultations, lectures and reports for the FCO, the Abu Dhabi government, Condé Nast Portfolio, Fortune and UNDP Somalia. His television and radio credits include WNYC, NPR and the Discovery Channel.

John W. Fox currently heads the Texas International Research Institute. He was formerly a professor of Anthropology and chair of the Department of Arab and International Studies at the American University of Sharjah and has held positions at the University of Pennsylvania, Union College and Baylor University, where he was chair of the Department of Anthropology for nineteen years. His writing deals with lineage-based states, political/religious movements in various parts of the world and he has studied how notions of time have been reformulated for the social relations of globalism in the epistemology of the social sciences. He has written two books on segmentary states and political anthropology and a further two books that examine how the Mayan cultural identity has been reformulated for global contexts. His articles have appeared in *Current Anthropology*, *The American Anthropologist* and *American Antiquity*, among others, and he has contributed chapters to numerous academic works. He serves on the editorial board of the *Journal of Social Affairs*, and was president of the Central Texas Archaeological Society for fifteen years, when he edited their journal.

Amr Hamzawy is a noted Egyptian political scientist who is currently working as Senior Associate at the Carnegie Endowment for International Peace, but taught previously at Cairo University and the Free University of Berlin. Dr Hamzawy has a deep knowledge of Middle East politics and specific expertise on the reform process in the region. His research interests include the changing dynamics of political participation in the Arab world and the role of Islamist opposition groups in Arab politics, with special emphasis on both Egypt and the Gulf countries.

Dr Hamzawy's studies at Cairo University focused on civil society and democratisation in the Arab world, Islamism and the cultural impacts of globalisation on Muslim majority societies. He received his PhD from the Free University of Berlin, where he worked as an assistant professor at the Centre for Middle Eastern Studies.

Sulayman Khalaf is currently Associate Professor of Social/Cultural Anthropology at the University of Bahrain. A Syrian anthropologist, he obtained his BA and MA from the American University in Beirut, and his PhD from UCLA. He has twenty-four years of teaching experience at AUB, UCLA, Kuwait, Stockholm and UAE universities, as well as a year at Harvard University as a visiting research scholar. He has carried out extensive research covering two important areas of contemporary Arab society: river 'water societies' (the Euphrates region in Syria) and 'oil societies' (the Gulf region). He is particularly interested in the impact of globalisation on Gulf societies, and issues revolving around modernity, state, identity and heritage revival. His focus is on the evolution of the oil state as a particular political type, as a modernising agent as well as a guardian of traditional and national cultural heritage. He has published extensively in English and Arabic, and his current research interests include the reconstruction of local culture and transnational migration within the Gulf.

Fred H. Lawson is Rice Professor of Government at Mills College, where he has taught International Relations and Middle East Politics since 1985. He is author of *Constructing International Relations in the Arab World* (2006), *Why Syria Goes to War* (1996), *Bahrain: The Modernization of Autocracy* (1989), and other studies of political economy and foreign policy in the contemporary Middle East. In 1992–3 he was Fulbright Lecturer in International Relations at the University of Aleppo; in the spring of 2001 he was Fulbright Lecturer in Political Science at Aden University.

Nada Mourtada-Sabbah is Associate Professor of Political Science and International Studies and Chair of the Department of International Studies at the American University of Sharjah (AUS). She received her PhD in Public Law with distinction from the University of Paris II, where she is a faculty associate at the Thucydides Center for Research and Analysis in International Relations. She was also recently appointed a faculty fellow in the Center for Congressional and Presidential Studies at American University (Washington, DC). Her books include *Le Privilège de l'Exécutif aux Etats-Unis*, *Les Tribunaux Militaires aux Etats-Unis*, and *Is War a Political Question?*, with Louis Fisher. She has co-edited a volume on *Globalization and the Gulf* and a volume on *The Supreme Court of the United States* and the *Political Question Doctrine*. Dr Mourtada-Sabbah has contributed to many eminent journals and is a member of the scientific board of the French journal *Politique Américaine* and serves on the editorial boards of the *Annuaire Français de Relations Internationales* and *Maghreb Mashrek*. She also serves as the deputy editor-in-chief of the *Journal of Social Affairs*, a peer-reviewed quarterly journal of the American University of Sharjah and the Sociological Association of the UAE, for which she initiated the English-language section.

Dr Mourtada has held visiting appointments at the University of California at Berkeley (Institute of Governmental Studies), the Congressional Research Service (Library of Congress), the University of Michigan at Ann Arbor (Department of Political Science) and the Institut d'Etudes Politiques de Paris (Sciences Po). Dr Mourtada was elected President of the Faculty Senate of the American University of Sharjah for the term 2003–4. She is a recipient of the AUS Excellence in Teaching Award and the AUS Excellence in Service Award.

Nimah Ismail Nawwab is an English writer, photographer, activist, lecturer and internationally recognised poet. Educated in Saudi Arabia, she is considered a trailblazing writer and poet. Her interests in diversity, change, tolerance, women's issues and empowering youth have led to involvement in various activities and presentations. Throughout these various activities she seeks to build bridges of understanding, and was recently dubbed a 'cultural ambassadress' and a 'voice for Arab women' based on a range of interactive readings and presentations in various countries across the East and West.

Her poetry has been published on several websites, translated into numerous languages, included in anthologies and taught at schools and colleges in Arabia, the US, Canada, Singapore, Japan and India.

She is also a poetry judge and facilitator of poetry sessions in several countries. The first Saudi Arab woman poet to be published in the United States, her pioneering work includes a historic, first-of-its-kind public book signing in Arabia and another in Washington DC. She is currently working on two anthology projects revolving around women and youth.

Nadia Rahman, who holds an MFA in Film and Video Production from the University of Wisconsin, has worked at the al-Jazeera satellite channel as a senior producer, director and news editor based in Washington DC where she covered 9/11 and its aftermath (2001–3). While living in Jerusalem during most of the 1990s, she worked as the senior producer for the BBC, covering the Middle East for news and current affairs programmes on television and radio. Prior to that, she was a producer for NHK (the Japanese Broadcasting Corporation) and CNN. She edited the Middle East section of *Gulf News* English daily out of Dubai, UAE, for a stint of six months. While a Fulbright Research Scholar in 2004, Ms Rahman researched a documentary on 'The Oral History of Elders in the UAE'. She currently holds an assistant professor position in the College of Communication and Media Sciences at Zayed University in the UAE, and is also the director of the Zayed University Media Center.

Ms Rahman's work has been recognised by Amnesty International, the Royal Television Society, Monte Carlo Television Awards and New California Media, among others. She continues to freelance as a journalist; most recently she published an article entitled 'In UAE, Tradition Yields to Times' in the *Washington Post*, with Pulitzer Prize-winning journalist, Anthony Shadid.

Robert Springborg completed a PhD in Political Science from Stanford University in 1974. Since that time he has held academic positions at Macquarie University in Sydney, Australia, the University of California, Berkeley, the University of Pennsylvania, and at the University of Sydney. In the late 1990s he served as Director for the

Middle East for Development Associates and was based in Cairo. From 2000 until 2002 he was Director of the American Research Center in Egypt. In 2002 he was appointed the MBI Al Jaber Chair in Middle East Studies at the School of Oriental and African Studies and Director of the London Middle East Institute.

Tim Walters is an Associate Professor of Mass Communication at the American University of Sharjah. He received his PhD in journalism from the University of Texas at Austin, where he was also a special student at the School of Law. Prior to joining the American University of Sharjah, Dr Walters taught at Zayed University.

Bibliography

Abdulla, Adnan K. and Hasan M. al-Naboodah, eds, *On the Folklore and Oral History of the United Arab Emirates and Arab Gulf Countries*, al-'Ain 2004.

Al-Anba Al-Kuwaitiyya, 8 August 1989.

Al-Haddad, Yahya, *Major Trends Affecting Families: A Background Document*, Report for United Nations, Department of Economic and Social Affairs, Division for Social Policy and Development, Programme on the Family, 2005.

Al-Ittihad newspaper, 12 September 1994.

Al-Kazi, Lubna, 'Divorce a Structural Problem not Just a Personal Crisis', *Journal of Comparative Family Studies*, University of Calgary, vol. 38.

Al-Refa'i, Hissa, *Songs of the Sea: A Study in Folklore* (in Arabic), Kuwait 1985.

Al Rumaihi, Mohammad, *Obstacles of Social and Economic Development in Contemporary Arab Gulf Societies* (in Arabic), Kuwait 1977.

Al Seyasah daily, 8 August 1989.

Al-Sharan International Consultancy, *United Arab Emirates Country Report*, Dubai 2001.

Alsharekh, Alanoud, ed., *The Gulf Family: Kinship Policies and Modernity*, London 2007.

Al-Watan, 13 August 1989.

AME Info, 'Expanding the City Centre', http://www.ameinfo.com/cgi-bin/cms/limit_country.cgi?ID=3190;Country=United%20Arab%20Emirates, 2005.

Amin, H. Y., 'Social Engineering: Transnational Broadcasting and its Impact on Peace in the Middle East', *Global Media Journal*, vol. 2, no. 4, 2004.

Anani, Ahmad, and Ken Whittingham, *The Early History of the Gulf Arabs*, London 1986.

Anderson, Benedict, *Imagined Communities*, London 1991.

Appadurai, A., *Modernity at Large: Cultural Dimensions of Globalization*, Minneapolis, Minnesota 1991.

'Arab Liberalism and Democracy in the Middle East,' *Middle East Review of International Affairs*, vol. 8, no. 4, 2004.

Azhary, M.S. El, ed., *The Impact of Oil Revenues on Arab Gulf Development*, London 1984.

Bairner, Alan, *Sport, Nationalism, and Globalization: European and North American Perspectives*, New York 2001.

Bandura, A., *Social Learning Theory*, Englewood Cliffs, New Jersey 1976.

Bandyopadhyay, Kausik, 'Prologue: The Real Peoples Game', *Soccer and Society*, vol. 7, nos 2–3/April–July 2006.

Barber, Benjamin R., *Jihad vs. McWorld*, New York 1995.

Bardsley, D., '"Terrible" Buildings Fail To Inspire Top Designers', *Gulf News*, 15 February 2005.

Barwind, J., and T. Walters, 'Swimming in the Bio-Cultural Soup: The Cell Phone and Society in the UAE', Theoretical Approaches and Practical Applications, Russian Communication Association, Rostov-na-Donu, 24–28 May 2004.

Ben-Porat, Amir, 'Split Loyalty: Football-cum-Nationality in Israel', *Soccer and Society*, vol. 7, nos 2–3 April–July 2006.

Benoist, Anne, 'Excavations at Bithna, Fujairah: First and Second Seasons', in Hellyer and Ziolkowski, eds, *Emirates Heritage*, vol. 1, al-'Ain 2005.

Bharadwaj, V., 'It's Essentially a Boy's Toy', *Gulf News*, Tabloid section, 10 March 2005.

Blandford, Linda, *Oil Sheikhs: Inside the Supercharged World of the Petrodollar*, London 1977.

Brown, J. S., and P. Duguid, *The Social Life of Information*, Boston, Massachusetts 2002.

Bullock, John, *The Gulf: A Portrait of Kuwait, Qatar, Bahrain and the UAE*, London 1984.

Burrows, Bernard, *Footnotes in the Sand: The Gulf in Transition, 1953–1958*, Salisbury, UK 1990.

Burton, R., *Personal Narrative of a Pilgrimage to Al Madinah and Mecca (Volume 1)*. Mineola, New York 1964.

Cole, Donald P., 'Where Have the Bedouin Gone?' *Anthropological Quarterly*, no. 76, Spring 2003.

Davidson, Christopher M., *The United Arab Emirates: A Study in Survival*, Boulder 2005.

——, 'The Emirates of Abu Dhabi and Dubai: Contrasting Roles in the International System', *Asian Affairs*, vol. XXXVIII, no. 1, 2007.

——, 'After Sheikh Zayed: The Politics of Succession in Abu Dhabi and the United Arab Emirates', *Middle East Policy*, vol. XIII, no. 1, 2006.

Dresch, Paul, 'Societies, Identities and Global Issues', in Paul Dresch and James Piscatori eds, *Monarchies and Nations: Globalisation and Identity in the Arab States of the Gulf*, London 2005.

Dubai Department of Ports and Customs, 'Dubai: non-oil foreign trade', in Dubai Department of Economic Development, *Development Statistics*, Dubai 2002.

Dubai Department of Industry, 'Jebel Ali Free Zone', *Dubai Department of Economic Development Statistics*, 2003.

Dubai Department of Tourism and Commerce Marketing, 'Hotels and Tourists', in *Dubai Department of Economic Development Statistics*.

Dunaway, David K. and Willa K. Baum, *Oral History: An Interdisciplinary Anthology*, Blue Ridge Summit, PA 1996.

Economic and Social Commission for Western Asia, *Women and Men in the Arab Countries: Employment*, Escwa/Stat/2002/2, 28 March 2002.

Economist Intelligence Unit, *United Arab Emirates*, London 2001.

Ewen, S., and E. Ewen, *Channels of Desire: Mass Images and the Shaping of American Consciousness*, 2nd edition, Minneapolis, Minnesota 1992.

Fakhreddine, J.H., 'Who Needs the Arabic Language?' *Gulf News*, section 1, 23 December 2004.

Fenelon, Kevin, *The United Arab Emirates: An Economic and Social Survey*, London 1973.

Fox, John W., Nada Mourtada-Sabbah, and Mohammed al-Mutawa, 'Heritage Revivalism in Sharjah', in *Globalization and the Gulf*, John W. Fox, Nada Mourtada-Sabbah, and Mohammed al-Mutawa, eds, London 2006.

——, 'The Arab Gulf Region: Traditionalism Globalized or Globalization Traditionalized?', in *Globalization and the Gulf*.

Fukuyama, Francis, 'Identity and Migration', *Prospect*, February 2007.

Gause, Gregory F. III, *Oil Monarchies: Domestic and Security Challenges in the Arab Gulf States*, New York 1994.

Geertz, Clifford, ed., *Old Societies and New States*, New York 1963.

Gellner, Ernest, *Nations and Nationalism*, New York 1983.

Gender Statistics Programme in the Arab Countries, http://www.escwa.Org.Lb/Gsp/Statistics/Main.html.

Gladwell, M., *The Tipping Point*, New York 2002.

Gruneau, R., 'Making Spectacle: A Case Study in Television Sports Production' in L. Wenner, ed., *Media, Sports and Society*, London, 1989.

Heard-Bey, Frauke, *From Trucial States to United Arab Emirates*, London 1982.

Held, Colbert C., *Middle East Patterns: Places, Peoples, and Politics*, Boulder, Colorado 1989.

Hellyer, Peter and Michele Ziolkowski, 'Introduction', in P. Hellyer and M. Ziolkowski, eds, *Emirates Heritage*, vol. 1, al-'Ain 2005.

Hilal, Ahmed, 'Excavations at Qarn al-Harf 67, Ras al-Khaimah, 2001', in P. Hellyer and M. Ziolkowski, eds, *Emirates Heritage*, vol. 1, al-'Ain 2005.

Hobsbawm, Eric, 'Introduction: Inventing Traditions' in E. Hobsbawm and T. Ranger, eds, *The Invention of Tradition*, Cambridge 1997.

Houchang, Chehabi, 'The Politics of Football in Iran' in *Soccer and Society*, vol. 7, nos 2–3 April–July 2006.

Hroch, Miroslav, *Social Preconditions of National Revival in Europe*, New York 2000.

Huntington, Samuel P., *Who Are We? The Challenges to America's National Identity*, New York 2005.

Hurreiz, Sayyid Hamid, *Folklore and Folklife in the United Arab Emirates*, London 2002.

Hutchinson, John, *The Dynamics of Cultural Nationalism*, London 1987.

Ibrahim, Youssef, 'Can Culture Be Bought in the Gulf?' *The New York Sun*, 5 February 2007.

Irish, John 'Gulf Investments in Sports, Games Theory', *MEED*, vol. 50, no. 41, 13–19 October 2006.

Ismail, Jaqueline, *Kuwait: Social Change in Historical Perspective*, Syracuse

1982.

Janardhan, N., 'GCC Countries Evolve Sporting Way to Success, Gulf Research Centre Analysis 3 December 2006. available at: http://www.arabnews.com/ ?page=6&section=0&article=89224&d=27&m=11&y=2006.

Jendli, A. and M. Khalifa, 'Effects of Western-Style Arabic Music Video Clips on Emirati Youth Identity and Culture,' International Academy for Media Science Conference, Arab Satellites in a Changing World, Cairo, Egypt June 2004.

Kennet, Derek, *The Towers of Ras al-Khaimah*, Oxford 1995.

Khalaf, Sulayman, 'Gulf Societies and the Image of Unlimited Good', *Dialectical Anthropology*, vol. 17, 1992.

——, 'Poetics and Politics of Newly Invented Traditions in the Gulf: Camel Racing in the United Arab Emirates', *Ethnology*, vol. 39, no. 3, Summer 2000.

——, 'Globalization and Heritage Revival in the Gulf: An Anthropological Look at Dubai Heritage Village', *Journal of Social Sciences*, vol. 19, no. 75, Fall 2002.

Kumaraswamy, P.R., 'Who Am I? The Identity Crisis in the Middle East', *The Middle East Review of International Affairs*, vol. 10, no. 1, Article 5, March 2006, available at: http://meria.idc.ac.il/journal/2006/issue1/Kumaraswamy.pdf

Lawless, R. I., ed., *The Gulf in the Early 20th Century: Foreign Institutions and Local Responses*, Durham 1986.

Leerssen, Joep, 'Nationalism and the Cultivation of Culture', *Nations and Nationalism*, no. 12, October 2006.

——, 'The Cultivation of Culture: Towards a Definition of Romantic Nationalism in Europe', *Working Papers in European Studies* number 2, University of Amsterdam 2005.

Lofgren, Orvar, 'The Nationalization of Culture', *Ethnologia Europaea*, vol. 19, 1989.

Luciani, Giacomo, 'Allocation vs. Production States: a Theoretical Framework', in H. Beblawi and G. Luciani, eds, *The Rentier State*, London 1987.

Mchombo, Sam, 'Sports and Development in Malawi', *Soccer and Society*, vol. 7, nos 2–3 April–July 2006.

McLuhan, Marshall, *The Guttenberg Galaxy*, New York 1969.

Messner, Michael, *Power at Play: Sports and the Problem of Masculinity*,

Boston 1992.

Moghadam,Valentine M., *Modernizing Women: Gender and Social Change in the Middle East*, Boulder 2003.

Mourtada-Sabbah, Nada, John W. Fox, and Mohammed al-Mutawa, 'Le syncrétisme entre capitalisme et traditionalisme dans le Golfe arabe', *Le Golfe Arabique entre capitalisme et tradition*, edited by Nada Mourtada-Sabbah, John W. Fox and Mohammed al-Mutawa, *Maghreb-Machrek*, no. 187, Paris 2006.

Nawwab, Nimah Ismail, *The Unfurling*, Selwa Press, California 2004.

Onley, James, 'Transnational Merchants in the Nineteenth-Century Gulf: the Case of the Safar Family', in Maadawi Al-Rasheed, ed., *Transnational Connections and the Arab Gulf*, London 2004.

Ouf, Ahmed M. Salah, *Urban Conservation Concepts for the New Millennium in the United Arab Emirates*, al-'Ain 2000.

Parents Television Council, 'Family TV Guide, *Extreme Makeover*', http://www.parentstv.org/ptc/shows/main.asp?shwid=1678, n.d.

Potts, Daniel, Hasan al Naboodah and Peter Hellyer, eds. *Archaeology of the United Arab Emirates*, London 2003.

Poulton, Emma, 'Mediated Patriot Games, The Construction and Representation of National Identities in the British Television Production of Euro '96', *International Review for the Sociology of Sport*, vol. 39, no. 4, 2004.

Preston, P. W., *Political/Cultural Identity Citizens and Nations in a Global Era*, London 1997.

Rahman, Nadia, Interview with Ahmed Rashid al Thani, Dubai, United Arab Emirates, November 2003.

Robins, Philip, *The Future of the Gulf: Politics and Oil in the 1990s*, Brookfield, Vermont 1989.

Sayyid Hamid Hurreiz, *Folklore and Folklife in the United Arab Emirates*, London 2002.

'Serious Work and Play for Gulf Monarchies' Elite Youth', *Gulf States Newsletter*, vol. 31, issue 797, 9 January 2007.

Simons, Char 'Doha's Grand Games', *Saudi Aramco World*, March/April, 2007, pp. 24–35.

Smith, Anthony D., *Nationalism and Modernism*, London 1988, p. 56.

Soffan, Lina U., *The Women of the United Arab Emirates*, London 1980.

Stent, M., 'Be Bold in Tackling Issues, Mohammed Tells Media' in *Gulf News*, 10 January 2005.

——, 'Confines of Law Must Be Eliminated,' *Gulf News*, 10 January 2005.

Swan, S., and T. Walters, 'A People in Transition?' unpublished manuscript, Dubai 2004.

Taryam, A. O., *The Establishment of the United Arab Emirates, 1950–85*, London 1987.

Thesinger, W., *Arabian Sands*, New York 1991.

Thomson, S., 'Dubai To Become Retail Category Killer', Retail International Surveys, http://www.retailinternational.co.uk/survtwo.htm, 2004.

Tomkins, Stephen, 'Matches Made in Heaven', *BBC News*, available at: http://newsvote.bbc.co.uk/mpapps/pagetools/print/news.bbc.co.uk/2/hi/uk_news/magazine/3828767.stm.

Velde, Christian, 'The Residence of Falayah', in P. Hellyer and M. Ziolkowski, eds, *Emirates Heritage*, vol. 1, al-'Ain 2005.

Vine, Peter, and Paula Casey, *United Arab Emirates: Heritage and Modern Development*, London 1992.

Walker, J., 'The Bedu, Towns and Rulers in the Emirates, 1920–1970', Bedouin Society in the Emirates, Center for Documentation and Research, Abu Dhabi, 26 February–1 March 2005.

Walters, T., 'Attitudes of Zayed University Students,' unpublished manuscript, Dubai 2003.

——, and Walters, L., 'The Social Consequences of Media Life Among Students in the UAE', Second International Conference on Communication and Mass Media', Athens Institute for Education and Research, Athens, Greece, accepted for presentation 2004.

——, Quinn, S., and A. Jendli, 'Media, Culture, and Society: The Roadmap to Life. Modernization, Globalization, and Cross-Cultural Communication', Tenth International Conference on Cross-Cultural Communication, Taipei, Taiwan, July 2005.

Wegner, D., 'Transactive Memory in Close Relationships,' *Journal of Personality and Social Disorder*, vol. 6, 1991.

Whiteoak, J., N. G., Crawford, and R. H., Mapstone, *Work Values and Attitudes in an Arab Culture*, Dubai 2004.

Wilson, J. W., and G. L Kelling, 'Broken Windows: The Police and Neighborhood Safety', *The Atlantic Monthly*, vol. 269, no. 3, 1982.

Winder, Robert, 'The Lost Tribes', *New Statesman*, 21 June 2004. Also available at http://www.newstatesman.com/20040621003.

Yamani, Mai, *Cradle of Islam: The Hijaz and the Quest for an Arabian Identity*, London 2004.

Ziolkowski, Michele, and 'Abdullah Suhail al-Sharqi, 'Bayt Sheikh Suhail bin Hamdan al-Sharqi, al-Fara, Fujairah, United Arab Emirates (preliminary study)', in P. Hellyer and M. Ziolkowski, eds, *Emirates Heritage*, vol. 1, al-'Ain 2005.

Index

About the London Middle East Institute

The London Middle East Institute (LMEI) of SOAS is a charitable, tax-exempt organisation whose purpose is to promote knowledge of all aspects of the Middle East, both among the general public and to those with special interests in the region. Drawing on the expertise of over seventy SOAS academic Middle East specialists, accessing the substantial library and other resources of SOAS, and interacting with over 300 individual and corporate affiliates, the LMEI since its founding in 2002 has sponsored conferences, seminars and exhibitions; conducted training programmes; and undertaken consultancies for public and private sector clients. The LMEI publishes a monthly magazine – *The Middle East in London* – and with Saqi it publishes four books annually in the SOAS Middle East Issues series. These activities are guided by a Board of Trustees on which is represented SOAS, the British Academy, the University of London, the Foreign and Commonwealth Office and private sector interests.

Professor Robert Springborg

MBI Chair in Middle East Studies
Director, London Middle East Institute
School of Oriental and African Studies
Russell Square, London WC1H 0XG
United Kingdom

www.lmei.soas.ac.uk